RYAN !

YOU ARE TRULY A MAN
WHO CARRY'S THE FATHER'S
LOVE.

Blessings)

One man's journey through hell
to find the truth about the truth.

MUD,
BLOOD
and
CARDBOARD

RUDY TRUSSLER

Published by Rudy Trussler
Eureka CA
info.rudytrussler@gmail.com

Editor: Anna G. Trussler
Cover and Layout Designer: Delaney-Designs

Library of Congress Control Number: 2012915499
ISBN-13: 978-0-9882461-0-2
ISBN-10: 0988246104

DEDICATION

This book is dedicated to my three children, Breanna, Aaron and Rebekah. You have walked every step of this journey with me and Mom without question. You defended us, carried us and ran with us. Without the three of you, I don't know if we would have survived. You are all equally my greatest source of inspiration and strength. It is a privilege and honor that you call me Dad.

CONTENTS

ACKNOWLEDGMENTS

The book you now hold in your hand started out as a simple record of a very personal and difficult time in my life while searching for healing. I wrote it intending for no one else to read it but me. When I shared it with my wife and then some friends, they lovingly prodded me until it morphed into a book project. Finishing it could not have happened without the help and encouragement of some incredibly amazing people to whom I want to express my gratitude and love.

First, there is Rachele Rickert who volunteered to read through my very first and very rough drafts. Your direct but kind input gave me the courage to continue writing.

Anna Grace, my favorite daughter-in-law, should get the editor's Purple Heart medal. She selflessly sifted through my manuscript several times with grace and poise even when I was not so poised. Thanks for not letting me burn my manuscript and for telling me what I needed to hear and not what I wanted to hear.

Jud Wilhite and Central Christian Church, choosing to love me and not to judge me, and showing me that it was "okay not to be okay" brought insurmountable healing. I am forever indebted to you for giving me and my family a place to be safe.

Ron and Cheri Gollner, I have said many times, "This is all your fault." I really mean that. You both took my family in so that we could see that we had a destiny and could actually dream again. I am who I am today largely because of you.

R.G. Ryan, who fiercely encouraged me to write, believed in me when I had a hard time believing in myself, and let me learn to "walk" on my own two feet but never failed to be there when I stumbled. You will never know what coffee on Tuesday mornings meant to me.

Barry Young, my friend for thirty-one years and counting. You have enthusiastically supported me all these years and still graciously listen to all my creative drivel.

Willy Bowles and Marty Pronovost, who took a risk on me, gave me a place to start again and the freedom to flourish. Thanks for pushing me to be myself, teaching me not take things personally and empowering me to do things I never imagined I could do.

And finally to my wife, Anna, you are my hero. Your courage and strength blows my mind every day. Thanks for loving me through this and allowing me to share our story with the world.

CHAPTER 1

American Graffiti

It is funny to me how a simple sentence can change a life. A bumper sticker, graffiti on a wall, a commercial jingle or a clever anecdote can effectively describe a person's emotional state of bliss or misery. I suppose we can refer to these types of sayings found on t-shirts and such as a sort of American pop culture, post-modern philosophy. You know, the sayings like:

- "Anything worth doing should have been done by now."
- "Sixty percent of the time it works every time."
- "Some days you're the dog and some days you're the hydrant."
- "The truth is out there, but I forgot the URL."

I guess these modern proverbs that we find on the backs of cars and scrawled across clothing are supposed to be amusing, but sometimes they can be a little too real. I encountered one of those life-changing bumper-sticker idioms in the summer of 2006 that set me on a quest to find the truth about the truth.

It was at a point in my life when my mind was racing with questions. Questions like, "Who have I become and why don't I recognize myself? How did I get to this desperate place?" I had no peace, just questions. Over a period of about ten years, those who had been commissioned to breathe life had betrayed me, lied to me, abandoned me and murdered my spiritual identity.

I was a lost soul looking for answers. I had been told that if I did the right things and said the right things, my life would be blessed and happy. I kept trying to use an equation that did not work. The religious "Christian formula" had failed. I was a former pastor living in Las Vegas, working construction. I was not happy and I did not feel blessed at all. I was miserable.

Then something happened. On a warm summer day, as I walked across a construction site in Las Vegas, I saw it. It was inked onto a port-a-potty wall and it stopped me in my tracks. The box of pipe fittings I was carrying fell to the ground. My mind zeroed in on the words despite the clatter of pipe parts crashing to the earth. It was like there was no other object in the world.

It was a single sentence – a question that captivated me. I think the author of this question was trying to be funny. However, I didn't find it amusing. I felt the sting of the question. I repeated it out loud. Written in thick, black, bold letters, it said:

"Is this all just a joke, or is God doing this to us on purpose?"

I stood there staring at the question, repeating it over and over again. It summed up my feelings. I needed to know the answer. I wanted to know why I went through what I did. I wanted to know why I was hard and bitter. I wanted to know if there was a God. If there was, was He truly a loving God, or just a mean kid with an ant farm and a magnifying glass? I needed to know the truth about the truth. Not the man-made formula, or the dos and don'ts, or what tradition said.

I guess that was the beginning. That day marked the start of the rediscovery of myself and a rediscovery of what it means to be a follower of Christ.

My wife Anna and I have weathered many storms and many turbulent situations together. She was diagnosed bipolar. This, mixed with betrayal and other very painful situations, sent us on a journey that can only be described as going through Hell.

On life's journey, no one chooses the difficult or painful path. It just happens. It's like one day you look down for a second, and when you look up, a sign says, "Now entering Hell." The next thing you know, you are experiencing the insufferable.

You might be going through your own version of Hell right now, and if you are not, chances are you just may someday.

Life just happens, and sometimes it happens hard. Anna and I have learned that there is more to life than just suffering through life's bad times. We have sifted through the garbage. We have been up to our necks in the muck and debris of life, and we survived.

I want to share our story with you: what we have experienced and how the answers about life, God and Christianity came to us. Then maybe we will discover the "truth about the truth." Perhaps we can answer the question: *Is this all just a joke or is God doing this to us on purpose?*

CHAPTER 2

It Was the Worst of Times (No, it was even worse than that!)

I was working as a youth pastor in California in February 1997, when the phone call came in. It was from Anna. I didn't know that she was about to set my world on its end. If I had known, I probably never would have answered the phone.

"Hi honey!" I said.

The voice on the other end was somber and careful.

"Rudy, I have to go to the hospital. I was just at the doctor and he said that I should go."

I was completely stunned by the news.

"What's wrong? Why do you have to go?" I asked, a bit confused.

Anna was not in the mood for a lot of questions. She had been seeing a psychiatrist for several months for depression, and he was the one sending her to the hospital.

"I have to go right now."

Puzzled, I asked, "What hospital?"

"I need to go to the psych hospital and I need to go now. I have someone to watch the kids, so please hurry."

"Yeah, but why do you have to go?"

"Rudy, I just need to go. I'll explain on the way."

I was off to take my wife of nearly nine years to the psych hospital. All I knew was that this was where crazy people went. Why was my wife going there?

The forty-five minute ride was awkward and confusing. I tried to figure out what was going on, but Anna's answers were vague. Between my confusion and her vague answers, I just gave up trying to understand.

We arrived at the hospital and checked Anna into what she would refer to as "The Funny Farm," even to this day. After filling out paperwork and taking care of insurance formalities, Anna and I were escorted upstairs to the Intensive Care Unit. There was a nurse's station and to the left of that station was an intimidating vault-like glass door.

The nurses inspected Anna's belongings and removed all products with alcohol, sharp objects and even the strings in her sweatpants. They removed her shoestrings from her shoes, turned to me and said, "Say your good-byes now." A quick kiss and a hug, and she disappeared into the glass vault.

There I stood in the hospital waiting area, stunned. People around me just went about their business. No one else seemed to care that my world had just fallen apart. The nurses filed charts and answered phones. No one even gave me a second thought. I just stood there staring, clueless and fractured.

I wasn't sure about what had just taken place, so naturally, I asked the nurse at the station if she could tell me what was going on. She looked at me smugly and said, "We can't discuss her with you because you might be part of the problem."

She returned to her very important paperwork. I was hoping for some compassion and maybe an answer that might, at the very least, make me feel better. All I got was a snippy reply and a cold dismissal. She just let me stand there in shock and awe of the recent events.

I grabbed a quick look into the glass door and saw a woman in her forties, knees pulled up to her chest, rocking back and forth on a bench. That was topped by a tall man resembling Edward Scissorshands (without the scissors, of course) pacing slowly in a hospital gown.

"Holy moley!" I thought. "I can't believe my wife is in there!"

I left at the same pace as the Edward Scissorshands-man and with the same far-off stare, and drove home to my three children, ages six, five and two.

On the way home, I pondered the situation. I had no idea what was happening. Things looked bleak and confusion filled my mind. I just knew that my wife was in a mental hospital and that I was not allowed any information as to why. I couldn't believe the nurse's suggestion that I was part of the problem. I hadn't even known there was a problem.

I picked up my kids, fed them, got them into bed, and made a few phone calls. I had to arrange rides to school, call family members, and get someone to come and help me with the girls' hair in the morning. I was not very good with making ponytails and braids. I went to bed alone and totally overwhelmed.

It took three days for the paperwork, which allowed the hospital and doctor to release information to me, to go through. I remember the phone call from the doctor. This would be the second phone call in three days that would change my life.

"Mr. Trussler, this is Dr. White, returning your call," he said in a warm, cordial voice.

"Thank you for calling me back so promptly, doctor," I said sarcastically.

He asked, "How can I help you?"

"Well, I want to know why my wife has been hospitalized. What is wrong?"

He replied in a compassionate and gentle tone that can only be compared to a kindergarten teacher kissing a little kid's boo-boo. I would have been infuriated if his statement had not stunned me.

"Your wife is depressed and we felt it best that she go into a safe place for a while," he said. There was a long, uncomfortable pause because I was shocked and confused.

My voice trembled as I asked, "Safe from what exactly?" I was completely ignorant about why people with depression get hospitalized, and his answer was unexpected.

"Well… I suppose from herself. People with deep depression sometimes have suicidal feelings, and when this happens, we have to place them into care where they will be safe."

Again, the kindergarten teacher routine, but this time I was grateful for it. I had just been informed that my wife, my children's mother, was suicidal. I needed all the compassion I could get. My heart raced, my mind spun, my mouth went dry and my spirit was crushed. For a few moments, "suicidal" was the only word in the English language that I knew.

Dr. White continued to explain to me why it was a good idea to hospitalize Anna and that after a couple of days, things would return to normal. That was not exactly the truth, because Anna did not return home for thirty-one days.

CHAPTER 3

The Thirty-one Day Prelude— to a Kiss

nce upon a time… so the fairytale begins. I used to have one of those pseudo-fairytale lives. I was living my dream. I became a youth pastor at age twenty-five, which had been my dream since age fifteen. I completed a two-year Bible college program in nine months, which led to me becoming an ordained minister. After a couple of part-time positions, I was working full-time in youth ministry.

I was a lucky guy! I was happily married with three kids while working in a ministry that I truly loved. Life was happy. Life was bliss. Maybe too blissful, which blinded me to the obvious difficulty around me. I was asleep and oblivious. The town crier was saying, "All is well," and nothing was.

After the phone call from "Dr. Kindergarten," I had to step up and be both daddy and Mommy. I had a lot to learn, and I was getting a crash course in Mommy 101.

Over the next thirty-one days, I had a very full schedule. I had to do my job as a youth minister, which included, but was not necessarily limited to: the Tuesday-night Bible studies, the Wednesday-night youth services, Sunday school programs, seventh-grade through college-age, and the monthly special events for each age group: junior high, high school and college. I usually spoke on at least one Sunday night service a month. I was also the drama director for all the holiday outreaches, and the Easter musical was just a few weeks away. Not to mention all the weekly staff meetings, board meetings, and the meetings that planned more meetings, counseling appointments and (deep breath) unexpected emergencies that a teenager may experience.

These did not happen between 9 a.m. and 5 p.m. Most of this happened after office hours, and usually during the nights and weekends. In addition to my job, I had to do what Anna had done for the last nine years – keep a home and raise our children.

I stepped up to the plate and pinch-hit. The only problem was that I had no idea what she had done all those years. I had no idea how to do her job. I did not know who liked mustard on a sandwich and who wanted mayonnaise. I did not know what drawer in the dresser was for pants, shirts, or socks and undies.

I did not know that bath time was a ritual that required certain toys for each kid that were kept in a bucket next to the bath. My son liked his lying next to the tub, and the girls wanted theirs in the water before they got in. Oh, and little did I know that they all had to stay in until their fingers and toes were all wrinkled up. If they were to get out any sooner, the earth would fall right off its axis! I did not know that I was so uninvolved in my own children's lives. Now, one might think, "Come on, no dad knows that stuff!"

Well, let me tell you about what happened one night at bedtime. I was putting everyone to bed, and after tucking in my son, I went into my girls' room. They were both already in their bunk beds. I walked in and my youngest said, "Hey! Daddy is in our room!" as if I had never been in there! I realized I couldn't remember the last time I was in there with a purpose, like to tuck them in and pray with them.

Ring! Ring! Wake-up call! Your three-year-old just told you that you suck as a father! Time to pay attention, dad! I realized that night that a child's bedroom is not just a sanctuary; it is a part of who they are. As parents, if we have an opportunity or an invitation to enter their rooms, it is an invitation to know who they are and what they are all about. To this day, I make it a point to go into each of my kids' rooms often, read the stuff on the walls, look at the pictures and look at the mess.

The days that followed were rough. I had help from church members. A friend came over every morning just to do the girls' hair. A couple came over to clean up for me, and of course, as with every church, meals were not lacking.

In the evenings, I would make the drive to the hospital as often as I could. I was physically drained, and emotionally I was a train wreck. Working in the ministry, taking care of the kids, paying the bills and trying to make sense of the mental illness situation was not going well. I felt alone and confused. I was holding on by a thread. I naively believed that Anna would be getting over this depression thing soon enough and that my life would go back to normal.

My daughter's seventh birthday was in a few weeks, and planning a birthday party was completely overwhelming. I thought that it would be best just to postpone the birthday celebration until Anna came home. However, Anna wanted to make sure that the kids experienced life as normally as possible, so I planned a birthday party. The details on the party are fuzzy. All I remember is the party preparation. Anna tried to help as much as she could. She gave me directions on what to do, but she was not focused on birthday parties, even though she wanted to be there.

I think Anna had already sent the invitations, so all I had to do was pull the party off. I got the outfits washed and ironed, cleaned the house and made sure there was a fresh roll of toilet paper in the bathroom. I was doing all right until I realized that eight-year-old girls don't just eat cake and go home. Games! I needed games. I was off again to buy party games. Looking back, I find this a bit amusing, because I bought prizes for the games, but I didn't plan any games.

The party came and was a success. As the last kid exited my home, I should have experienced an overwhelming feeling of fulfillment. I didn't. I was exhausted. A house full of eight-year-old girls had just kicked my butt.

After a brief call to Anna to report on the party, I collapsed into bed. I wondered when she would be home. I realized that I needed her home because I sucked at her job. I thought for a minute that if she was to have a long-term bout with depression, I would not be able to handle it. I barely handled a birthday party. How was I going to handle everything else? I was terrified that my wife was crazy and never getting out of that place. I was scared for her safety! I begged God that night to give me my wife back, and if memory serves me correctly, I cried myself to sleep for the first time in my adult life.

"What a wuss," I thought to myself as my eyes closed.

Visitations to the Funny Farm in the early days were like *Mr. Rogers' Neighborhood* on Thorazine. Going to see my wife in a mental institution destroyed my nice, safe little world. This was not my life! This happened to other people. This was outside my box! My wife did not belong here! I did not belong here visiting her! I had never been so uncomfortable being anywhere in my life, but uncomfortable or not, I went there to see her.

On my first visit, I saw the same characters I had seen before. Edward Scissorshands-man was still there, so was fetal-position woman and the demons in nurses' clothing. Since a release had been signed and I proved that I was not part of the problem, the nursing staff was nicer to me, although still smug and unhelpful.

I was escorted into the big glass vault and Anna was waiting for me in the visiting area. She looked timid, almost embarrassed, and she hugged me and hung onto me tightly for a long time. I asked her how she was doing and she tried her best to make me feel good about her being there. The conversation was pleasant as she explained group therapy and daily activities. Then I asked her about her diagnosis. She explained it was Severe Depressive Disorder. I had no idea that my wife was experiencing such massive depression, and I felt like a fool for not recognizing the severity of her condition.

I don't know if you have ever had someone close to you tell you that he or she wants to take his or her own life, but I could never get used to the idea that the person I love wanted to take herself permanently away. I think the threat of suicide is just as damaging as the act itself. It causes fear and anguish that is nearly unmatched by anything I have ever experienced.

I have a very difficult time with the idea of suicide. I am more homicidal. I like me, and therefore I'd rather cause great bodily harm to the person irritating me than to hurt myself. When Anna explained her suicidal feelings, I had a very difficult time understanding her. It took years for me to fully comprehend how anyone could feel so badly that he or she would entertain the idea of suicide. In those days, all it did was scare me half to death, and that usually led to me getting angry at Anna. It seemed selfish for her to want to permanently remove herself from me and the kids.

The visit was nice, even though it did not put me at ease. Leaving was difficult. I wanted to take Anna home with me, but I had no choice but to leave her there. I felt alone as I walked to my car. I was helpless. I was at the mercy of the doctors and nurses of the Funny Farm. As I drove away, I prayed for Anna's safety and that she would be home soon. I went home to three kids. That night I got into an empty bed, but all four of us filled it by morning. Our house was not exactly home without Anna.

I have conversed with gays and lesbians, drug addicts, alcoholics and homeless people. Over the years, I have met every walk of life there is to meet in the mental health world. I have witnessed the paranoid and the psychotic. I have encountered people hearing voices as well as people answering the voices. I have met those who have cut themselves, scratched themselves and burned themselves, and suicidal men and women who have no hope at all. I have witnessed hospital staff wrestling patients to the ground to sedate them for their own safety and the safety of others. I never objected to this when I was in the room, and in fact, was ever so thankful!

In the latter part of the thirty-one days, I met a cast of characters that I would come to love, but who scared me in the beginning. The Edward Scissorshands-man and the fetal-position woman were just the opening act for this freak show. Inside a month's time, my wife had new friends.

There was a woman who had survived a brain aneurysm, was partially crippled and was in so much pain that she wanted to die. Another obsessed over the number three and was severely OCD. My favorite was a young lady who heard vivid voices telling her to burn herself. She burned her arms so badly that both of her forearms required skin grafting. In order to stretch the skin properly, the doctors had to place breast implants in her arms. One can imagine the huge, bulbous protrusions in her forearms. It looked as incredible as it sounds.

I met people with bandages on their slashed wrists, people medicated so badly that they could hardly speak, and people with bruised emotions and battered minds. I graciously accepted their company as I visited Anna, but I did not like that my wife was now one of them. She was the newest cast member of the greatest freak show on earth, and I had to accept them because I accepted her. I loved Anna and I slowly started to love them.

What I discovered was that this was no freak show. This was a gathering of hopeless, tortured souls, and the world had been cruel to them. Here they found kindness, belonging and acceptance, and no one judged them for being who they were. It was more normal than the rat race in the so-called normal world, full of rejection, manipulation, greed and selfishness. It was refreshing to watch.

Meanwhile, in the so-called normal world, the members of the church I served were busy with speculation and judgment.

CHAPTER 4

Reality Upside-Down Cake

Sometimes the simple, daily conversations that we can have with just about anybody can shake your world off its proverbial axis. These discussions often have an opening sentence that will instantaneously take you off smoothly paved roads down the dirt roads of doom.

Hearing, "You're fired," after twenty years of faithful service will change your perspective slightly. The conversation beginning with, "I'm pregnant," will transform jet-skis and weekend getaways into diapers and Saturday morning cartoons in a mere nine months. The list is never-ending:

- "The test results are positive. You have cancer."
- "Mom, dad… I'm gay."
- "Will you marry me?"
- "I want a divorce."
- "Dad passed away."
- "Your loan has been approved."

In April 1997, I had a conversation like this. It began a chain reaction of events that would send my life splintering into several different directions in a very short time.

Anna came home after thirty-one days in the Funny Farm. I could tell that she was happy to be home, but there were a few things that were different. She seemed somewhat distracted and preoccupied. I let it go because I was happy to have her home and having her home and a little off her game was better than her being in the hospital.

Anna had just returned home from a visit with her psychologist when the conversation began. It was a strange conversation. Anna was talking in a very methodical and deliberate fashion. I knew she was serious, but she wasn't making any sense. Her conversation drifted around a little and then she started talking about what would happen if we didn't stay together. I had no idea what she was talking about, and I told her I had no intention of leaving. Then, as suddenly as lightning strikes, she got to the reason behind the conversation.

In the television show *Star Trek*, just before the Enterprise is about to have a collision, Captain Kirk would say, "Brace for impact!" I wish someone had been able to tell me to brace myself, because I was not prepared for the next part of the conversation. It was one of those statements that changed everything.

"I've been seeing someone."

If there is one word that describes hurt, shocked, angry and devastated all at once, I do not know what it is, but in a split second, I felt all of those emotions.

I asked, "Have you been intimate?"

"Yes," she replied as matter-of-factly as though she were saying, "We are out of milk."

I could hear the sound of glass breaking. It was my world crashing down around me. The details after this are cloudy, but I remember tears and kicking over the Fisher-Price kids' table in the kitchen.

Words flew, some of them unkind, but no name-calling or petty rhetoric. In a single instant, my life, family and ministry were in jeopardy because of her choice. Over and over in my head I kept thinking, "This isn't happening to me."

But it was happening. I was getting a full helping of reality upside-down cake and it was cold, undercooked and bitter. Then the questions came.

"I cried myself to sleep because of her?"

"I stuck by her through the depression and this is what I get?"

"I loved her forever and this?"

It was a Friday morning, my day off. The weekend would be very difficult, but not as difficult as the subsequent seven days.

The weekend was quite a ride – a long ride. Right after the conversation with Anna, I went into survival mode. Anna told me that she would end the affair and went to say her goodbyes. I went to visit friends and sought support. I went first to a friend who taught at a Christian school at church, and I got permission from the principal to pull her from class and help me with my emergency. We went and sat in a park for awhile and talked. I don't remember her saying anything specific. I just remember that she was able to make me feel calm. After getting my head back on somewhat correctly, I went to see my close friends, John and Elaine. John was a board member and Elaine was the director of music ministries. I went to their home and told them the news.

After prayer and more settling of my nerves, the next step was to go to my pastor and let him know that my marriage was in trouble. I didn't like the idea, but he was my boss and needed to know what was going on. He was also my pastor and I needed him to help me get through this. The church was helping a smaller church several miles away with some remodeling, and that was where my pastor was. John took the time to drive me to the church forty-five minutes away.

The ride was long and my heart was pounding. I knew exactly what was hanging in the balance. My ministry could be over as well as my marriage. The particular fellowship I was a part of didn't look too kindly on moral failure. Divorce was considered a moral failure, not to mention adultery. I had failure of some sort in every direction I looked. I was unsure, scared and bewildered. I had no idea what was going to happen next.

We pulled into the church parking lot in the mid-afternoon. I felt the warm air brush across my face as I got out of John's truck. I looked around and could see all sorts of people from the church working on the building. I could see the pastor on the roof. John said, "I'll go get him."

He went over and called him down. When Pastor Rich climbed down from the roof, John said, "Rudy has something he needs to talk to you about." My pastor walked up to me.

"Anna is having an affair," I blurted out uncontrollably. He hugged me with both arms. I cried and he just hugged me, hanging on like any good friend would, and he let me cry. He was not only my pastor, he was my mentor and he was being the good friend I needed.

He and I met when I was hired to be the youth pastor at First Church in southern California. He was the associate pastor at the time and it didn't take long for us to become friends. He soon became a mentor to me. Pastor Rich, Elaine and I became close friends when we struggled with the senior pastor, who had apparently lost his vision for the church. The three of us desperately tried to hold the church together during a very tumultuous time. We used to joke and call ourselves the three amigos.

Rich wanted to be the pastor of First Church, and Elaine and I wanted him to be. Eventually, the senior pastor resigned, my friend became pastor, and Elaine and I were on his staff. Rich had taken the time to sit and talk to me about life, the Bible, and books he had read. He taught me by example the importance of prayer and breathed into me a heart for the hopeless people in the world. He, in a way, taught me about being a pastor with a heart for people, not just a youth pastor with a heart for teens. My pastor, leader, mentor and close friend of four years was now holding me up in his arms while I sobbed.

"We are going to get through this," he said softly. "It's okay, and nothing is going to change. We are going to get through this."

We sat and talked for a while. I told him all of the details and that Anna had agreed to end the affair. I told him that I feared for my ministry.

"I am not going to let you go anywhere," he said. Those were his exact words.

We talked about the future and he suggested that I might take a sabbatical until there was some healing. He promised that I was staying on staff and that he would not let me leave. With that, I felt better about the situation and went home to mend my broken relationship with Anna.

CHAPTER 5

The Kiss

"One should rather die than be betrayed. There is no deceit in death. It delivers precisely what it has promised. Betrayal, though… betrayal is the willful slaughter of hope."

-Steven Deitz, American playwright

broken promise sometimes comes neatly wrapped in betrayal, and can be devastating. It is sometimes disguised in pure motives, but it is still betrayal. Like when people say, "Yes, our conversation was in confidence, but I told him what you said because he needed to hear it."

People have had a track record of disloyalty throughout history. Marcus Brutus betrayed and killed Julius Caesar. Benedict Arnold is best known for his sedition of the colonies by plotting to surrender the American fort at New York to the British. The most famous act of betrayal is Judas, who betrayed Jesus Christ with a kiss. Think about that for a moment. He betrayed him with a kiss. Such an act is so painful, I think, because it always comes with insult followed by injury.

After spending time with Rich that dark Friday afternoon, I went home knowing that I was going to be okay. Rich was my mentor and friend and I trusted him wholeheartedly. If Rich was in my corner, I was fine. I was safe and so was my ministry. The next seventy-two hours were like riding an emotional rollercoaster with all the curves and loops, only with no seat belt and a belly full of Thanksgiving dinner. I was hanging on for dear life and I was about to hurl.

That's what it felt like when I caught Anna on the phone with "him" while she was locked in the bedroom. I listened to the conversation outside the door. Anna hadn't really said goodbye. The confrontation that followed was awful.

"I don't love you," she said, looking at me with big, dark, empty eyes. "I don't want you, I don't want the kids or the ministry, and I just want to be with him."

There's nothing like a big helping of "I don't love you" from your wife to make you all warm inside. No, wait, it was all cold and it felt more like smashing your finger in a car door, except my whole body was smashed. I prepared myself for the worst possible scenario. I started to make peace with myself and tried to get comfortable with the idea of my marriage being over. I decided I had better get used to the idea of divorce.

I went for a drive Sunday afternoon and cruised the nearby hillsides overlooking the city. I wanted to get my head clear. I began to wonder about what would happen next. Would Anna and I divorce? Would I be okay raising three kids alone? Would any church hire a pastor who was a single dad? Who is going to want to be with a man with a failed marriage under his belt and three kids? Would I be alone forever? As I was thinking about it, the song "Independence Day" by Martina McBride began to play on the radio.

"Let freedom ring, let the white dove sing. Let the whole world know that today is a day of reckoning. Let the weak be strong, let the right be wrong. Roll the stone away, let the guilty pay. It's Independence Day."

The words made me feel that I was going to make it. I felt like the chorus applied to me, even though the song wasn't about my situation. For the first time in three days, I felt some peace. I thought to myself, "I am going to be okay. I am going to be okay!"

I parked the car and got out. I looked over the city below me. Cars moved up and down the streets and people were just living their lives as normal. Somewhere down there, my wife was plotting to leave me and the kids. Kids who were innocently playing, just being kids, and had no idea they were about to lose their mom to mental illness.

"Life is awesome," I said sarcastically under my breath. I actually laughed to myself at the absurdity of what my life was in that moment. I picked up a tree branch that reminded me of Moses' staff. My mood turned somber now as I began to pray. I asked for strength. My life was in a fog. I could only see a few feet in front of me and I was scared of what was ahead.

"So God, what do I do now?" I prayed. "I need your help now more than ever. I need your strength to get me through this."

I didn't feel any stronger, and if anything, I felt weaker. I stood there feeling like a fool. I expected some strength and I just got tired. I wanted to yell out, "Yo, Big Guy! What are you doing? I am fading out down here!" I didn't though. I just stood there, looking at the valley, playing with the tree branch. I looked at the ground, feeling hollow and empty. I watched a teardrop hit the ground, then several more, but I didn't feel myself crying.

"Help me, God," I whispered. "I have nothing left and I can't go on." It was one of the most desperate moments of my life. The tears fell more rapidly now and I still felt nothing. I was numb. I waited. For at least thirty minutes, I said and heard nothing. Tears rolled off my numb face and I thought I was losing my mind. I looked at my hand

and in it was the stick that reminded me of Moses' staff. At that moment, God touched my soul. In that way that only God can, He spoke to me in that tiny little voice in the back of my mind.

"What is that in your hand?" He asked. That was it. He asked me a question. I answered in my mind. "It's a staff." That was it. I knew what it meant. In the Bible, God asked Moses, "What is that in your hand?"

"A staff," Moses replied. It was just a walking stick to help him deal with the journey of life. He saw no special significance in it. However, the miraculous potential of that insignificant staff became clear when God told him to throw it on the ground and it became a snake. When God told Moses to pick up the snake by the tail, it turned back into a staff in his hand. Something simple and common turned into a powerful, authoritative tool, and then back to something simple and common.

When God finished showing Moses that his staff was an instrument of divine power and authority, it was all he needed to fulfill his task. Though there was no power in my tree branch, I believe God gave it to me as a symbol of His divine power and authority, and He was going to see me through. I threw the stick in the back of my truck and drove off to face the next phase of my life with the assurance that God was with me. I still have that stick today.

I stopped by to see Rich on my way home. He was getting ready to go to the evening service. I just wanted to say hello and see if he had anything encouraging for me. I explained what Anna had said, how I thought that my marriage was probably over, and that she was still calling the guy. Rich and his wife prayed with me, and Rich again reiterated that I was not going to have to resign and that we were going to focus on restoration. He told me again that I would probably take a sabbatical and that I would return to full service after some time. I told Rich and his wife that I wanted to make the relationship work and that Anna was sick and needed help. Rich's wife told me to be strong and that I should move forward, but that I should realize that my marriage would never be the same. I left their home bewildered, but God was with me.

That evening, Anna had a visit from a very special friend. Raychele is one of those people who has a spiritual mind, but has not lost touch with humanity. She has experienced life's kick in the teeth a few times and she just has a way of transforming life's random dung piles into blessings of gold. She spent the better part of an hour with Anna. I don't know what she said, but it just may have jump-started the reconfiguring of Anna's mind and spirit.

After Raychele left, I made tea, and Anna and I sat at the kitchen table and tried to talk. It was one of the most aggravating moments of my life. The conversation went nowhere. It was like trying to talk to a spoiled teenage debutante. She didn't want to talk, her mind was made up, and nothing I said was of any significance. I went to bed that night realizing that if God didn't step in and do something, we were done. I went to bed scared and anxious. I didn't think I'd sleep at all. I knew that God was on my side, but I was still nervous and felt a little sick. Surprisingly enough, I fell asleep and slept the entire night.

Monday morning, I awoke to Anna sitting at the edge of the bed, smiling down sweetly at me. She was completely changed. She no longer had dark, lifeless eyes… and pause! Yeah, go ahead and drink this in. It's weird and people don't just change overnight. She was different. Now this part of the story is personal, and all Anna and I can say is that God did intervene. He spoke in a way that He does and her mind was set right for the moment.

Back to the story. I was not exactly overwhelmed with joy. I was taken aback and didn't know whether she was looking for a good place to stick a knife or if I had dreamed the last three days. But there she was, sitting there smiling at me, and I was sort of smiling back.

Some may ask, "Why did He choose to do this in this place and time?" God does stuff like that, that's why. Here is what I have learned about God's love and intervention: When God responds to a situation, it has nothing to do with what we do. It is all about what God is doing. God is God and we are His children. God is good all of the time and God does good stuff all the time. It's just that simple.

Most people wanting a miracle are looking for a dramatic event to occur while the whole world watches as this extraordinary thing takes place. If we are looking for a virgin birth or a sea to part, we will miss the thing God is doing. I woke up and things were better, and it was because of God. There was no other explanation.

Anna was better and we talked about the next step of our lives. We had a lot of garbage to work through. Our issues did not get all worked out in a single conversation. We started the process that morning. It took time, but we decided to stick it out and make our marriage work.

It was now Monday. Three days had passed since the initial blow, and the next thing that we had to do was go and talk to Pastor Rich. I called the church office and set a time for Anna and me to come in that day. On the way to church, we discussed what we were going to say and how we were going to explain it. We decided on the truth and told him every detail of how God had restored Anna back to her senses. God spoke to Anna in a very real way and we shared this with Rich. He did not seem to believe us. I felt that something in him had changed. He said that he would pray about it and informed us that there was a board meeting that evening to discuss my "situation." My situation? I now had a situation. I had been upgraded from, "Don't worry; we'll get through this," to a "situation." In my mind, this was the equivalent of progressing from, "We have a little storm front" to "It's an F-5 tornado."

I left not knowing what was going to happen next. I was too exhausted to care. My ministry and career were now in the hands of a church board and what they thought about my "situation." Rich once again assured me that my job was not at stake and that we were going to be fine. To clear things up, this was not just "my job." This ministry and the youth group were my life. I had been there nearly five years and I had poured everything into that group of kids that I dearly loved. Being a youth pastor was not what I did. It was who I was. To consider this a "situation," as a mere matter of losing my job, seemed to trivialize it a bit.

Tuesday came and I had no idea what had happened at the board meeting that previous evening. I do not exactly remember who called whom, but I believe I got a call from Pastor Rich who asked to come and see us. The tone in his voice was cheerful; the kind of cheerful voice that was trying very hard to be cheerful. We set an appointment.

The next part of the story goes into some unpleasant detail and is almost surreal. Before I move on, I feel the need to clarify a few things. First, the purpose of this book is *not* to express bitterness, nor is it to get back at anyone. This book is *not*, and I repeat, *is not* about retribution. However, it is about finding peace in horrible and dreadful times. Secondly, I have long since forgiven people over the years, and though I am not friends with some of these people any longer, I do not have ill will or hold contempt against them. Lastly, I am not writing about these things to fuel some half-baked argument that everyone in the church is bad, or that Christians are horrible and hypocritical people. Christians can be horrible and hypocritical and let's face it, the church is an imperfect place. No need to argue. Read this and be amazed if you must, but this is not the good stuff. This part of the story is merely the sewage we have to wade through to get to the good stuff.

"The board has made the difficult decision to ask for your resignation," Pastor Rich said. He spoke deliberately. He was kind and tried to be fatherly. "We feel it would be best for you to resign rather than have to fire you. I will need a letter of resignation before tomorrow's service, and we will make an announcement then."

I considered the idea of being fired and realized that I was no longer going to be on staff. That's when my slow death began. I gave up right then and there. I quit and had no fight left. I agreed to write the letter.

"Why would you have to fire me?" I asked.

Rich looked at me in the best fatherly face he could muster.

"Because, after talking to the fellowship and the leaders of the denomination, we all agree that you have a very difficult road ahead of you," he said. "We all believe that it's better for you to heal and have your marriage restored while not being on staff."

Rich's tone became more serious with every word.

"Besides that, you will more than likely lose your credentials with the denomination," he said. "The church board unanimously agrees, and this is our decision."

Under normal circumstances I would have been devastated, but I was exhausted, embarrassed and I just wanted to run away.

"Look, Rudy," Rich continued. "I know this is hard, and I am going to still be here as your pastor and your friend, and I hope to continue to be a mentor to you."

After some brief pleasantries, hugs and prayer, he was on his way. The life I loved was over. I wrote my letter of resignation and even though no one asked her to, Anna wrote a letter explaining what she had done. It was a very difficult task. Wednesday night came and we found ourselves in the pastor's office for a short meeting with him and his wife, a half an hour before the midweek service.

I remember feeling numb. I didn't care what happened. I just wanted it to be over. I was exhausted. We walked from the office to the sanctuary using a side door. The place was packed. It was then that I learned that on Sunday, Pastor Rich had called for an informal business meeting, so the attendance was higher than usual for a Wednesday evening. The youth group was sitting on the right side of the church. I only looked in their direction briefly, and we took our seats in the front row of the church. I do not remember how the evening started. I think we sang some songs and then the pastor took the platform.

He greeted everyone and addressed the matter at hand quickly. Anna and I sat in the front row, listening as he told the entire congregation, including the youth group, that my wife had been involved in an adulterous affair and that I had resigned. He then read my letter of resignation before reading Anna's letter. We did not know that he was going to read her letter, and I did not know that he was going to expose to the whole world that Anna was an adulteress. Now, looking back, I don't remember what we were told about what was going to happen. I do remember feeling embarrassed and ashamed because my pastor, friend and mentor told the entire church that my wife had committed adultery and that I had chosen to resign.

My personal, private life had now been made public. But he lied. I did not choose to resign, I was told to resign by him and a church board that had voted unanimously that I should resign or they would fire me. *Smack!* And there was the kiss of betrayal.

"Et tu, Brute?" Perhaps the most famous three words uttered in literature. Even you, Brutus? Adultery is an ugly thing that rarely results in anything but a divorce. However, we survived. I had been given false hope that nothing was going to happen to me. In other words, my ministry was safe. I was going to have to take a sabbatical to renew my marriage. This made perfect sense to me, by the way. If my marriage was on the rocks, it would be better to have the time to repair what had been damaged. This would have been the ideal thing for the board to do. But this was not going to happen, was it? Do you remember the last promise made to me by my pastor, friend and mentor?

"Look, Rudy, I know this is hard, and I am going to still be here as your pastor and your friend, and I hope to continue to be a mentor to you."

Well, it didn't happen. After that Wednesday night church service, I never heard from the man again. I was left on my own to pick up the pieces of my life. There were no visits, no phone calls, nothing. This was the most difficult thing for me to deal with out of it all. Oh, and it was not just him. All those people who Anna and I had relationships with, the friends and the "brothers and sisters" in the Lord who had become a source of strength and family... gone. We were damaged goods, and no one wanted to deal with us. All those years working together and we were out. We were no longer in the church directory, no longer on the prayer chain. Just removed and cut out like a cancerous tumor. Only a small handful of people even bothered calling to check on us. Now, twelve years later, we have three families that keep in touch. Three families who have actually been there to see us survive and those three families were there to see us victorious. They will never know how much I appreciate them and their commitment and friendship.

But my pastor, friend and mentor just dropped me. Even when I called him, I did not get a return call. It was painful. I had just been directing the church Easter drama. I had just been speaking to my youth group the week before. I had just found out my wife was cheating on me and I was asked to resign my position as a youth pastor. I needed a little support! My life had just come crashing down around me, and I had to pick up the pieces alone. Was this even right? Was it even biblical? I only know one way to answer these questions:

> *"Dear brothers and sisters, if another believer is overcome by some sin, you who are godly should gently and humbly help that person back onto the right path. And be careful not to fall into the same temptation yourself. Share each other's burdens, and in this way obey the law of Christ" (Galatians 6:1-2).*

No, it was not biblical; it was wrong. This passage of scripture does not say, "Dear brothers and sisters... when you see someone in sin, cut them off, and if a brother needs help through a terrible time, leave him to fend for himself." That was just the beginning of the damage.

CHAPTER 6

Killing Me Softly

*"Hurt leads to bitterness, bitterness to anger, travel too far down
that road and the way is lost."*

--Terry Brooks

W e started the process of healing in one area and a process
of deterioration in another. The church had given us a
three-month severance package, which included benefits.
We had to use these three months to pick ourselves up and move on.

We spent hours together talking and we took small, one-day
vacations to Six Flags Magic Mountain. It would be insincere and
a blatant act of denial to pretend that we didn't have tons of garbage
to work through. We had to sift through a city landfill of refuse if
we were to survive, so we did what it took. We both stepped up and
cleared the garbage out.

It took us about a year to be set right again, but believe it or not,
we came out of the affair more in love; healed and renewed. A couple
of people have told me to write a book on how to survive an affair, but
honestly, I have no idea how we did it. It was painful at times, but I believe what made this work was that we both just hit all the issues head-
on and didn't side-step anything. We had to do something. We had
nothing but time and that made it easier to put the pieces back together.

As far as my next step in my career and ministry, I think deep down I was waiting for a phone call that would invite me back to First Church. I really loved that church. I loved the people and the teens I worked with, and I loved the pastor.

I am not sure exactly what was in the hearts and minds of the men that decided to dismiss me by requesting my resignation. I did not believe that anyone on the board was out to get me. At first, I believed that their motives were pure and their decisions were made in my best interest. I remember it actually being a bittersweet relief that I was resigning. It was easier. I could run away and hide.

Then I woke up one morning about two weeks later and I realized what I had done. I allowed things to happen that I did not agree with. It was not the congregation's business what had happened in my marriage. If I had been in my right mind, I would never have let my personal life be exposed the way it was on that Wednesday night. The sleeping giant inside me was awake but there wasn't a thing I could do about it.

I remember going to the park with my family. Anna and I were sitting on a park bench and watching our kids play. I remember feeling so hurt and angry. I usually would enjoy this time with the family, but I was miserable. I felt like a fool because I had let them force me to resign. I had allowed them to take advantage of me while I was still stunned from the news of my wife having an affair. I couldn't help but feel like Pastor Rich had done this on purpose, and that he knew exactly what he was doing. He had an agenda. It was at this very moment that the hurt began to slowly and steadily morph into anger. The weeks that followed only substantiated my feelings.

During that time, several board members contacted me to talk to me about the board meeting itself. The general theme was that Pastor Rich's agenda in the board meeting was to dismiss me. One board member's wife stopped by the house just to tell me that what was said at the Wednesday night service about a "unanimous" decision by the board to seek my resignation was not true. She came to tell me that her husband had not voted in favor of my resignation. He abstained from the vote altogether. He felt so bad about what had happened that he could not face me.

During a visit to a friend in the hospital, I bumped into another board member. He was sort of the "head of the board" at the time. He brought up the board meeting and we talked about what had happened for a few minutes. He wanted to know if I was doing all right and he especially wanted to know if Pastor Rich had been in contact with me. I told him emphatically, "No, not even a phone call."

He seemed disappointed. Either that or he had some other reason to stare at his shoes for the next few moments. I was able to ask him a few questions that he handled with grace and wisdom. He would not divulge any details as to who said what, but he did talk openly. I asked him, "Do you think that what happened was right?"

"No, I do not," he said. "But in the end we had to make a decision."

I guess it didn't matter if it was bad or someone got hurt; it was just necessary because they had to "make a decision."

I went to see my denomination's area leader to discuss my future. I explained to him what Pastor Rich had said – that he had already spoken to this office and that I would lose my credentials over Anna's affair. My area leader looked me right in the eye and said that was not true. I had done nothing wrong and would not lose my credentials. Then after encouraging us to keep going in the direction of renewing our marriage and telling us how impressed he was that we were doing the right thing, he said something that about knocked me over.

"Rudy," he said. "Just so you know, no one spoke to anyone in this office about you concerning this matter."

I was appalled. I couldn't believe what I was hearing. Pastor Rich had lied. My pastor, mentor and friend had lied to me.

The drive home was a quiet one. Neither Anna nor I had very much to say. The damage had been done, the lies had been told, and those who we thought cared for us the most had done the unspeakable. Anna and I had a very hard time digesting the fact that we had been treated this way. She dealt with it the best she could. She has always been a person to hold things close to her heart and sort of hide within herself. She did not say too much about it to me, but I knew that it was eating away at her mentally as well as emotionally.

I never understood why the board and Pastor Rich didn't consider my wife's mental state. It felt like it didn't matter to them. I felt like they didn't care. I later found out that it might have been because Pastor Rich did not believe that Anna was suffering from any type of mental disorder at all. I later found out that he had told several people that he believed that she was acting out for attention.

Anna asked me in tears several times why he did what he did. I had no answers. The person who did have the answers had decided to ignore us. What does a person even say to this? What does a person do? Where does he turn? I didn't know the answers to these questions, so I said and did nothing except think about it day and night. I didn't realize it at the time, but the unresolved situation started to fester within me. It wasn't long until bitterness set in like gangrene and infected my soul with a disease that corroded and choked out my spirit.

CHAPTER 7

The Tribe Has Spoken

I am drawn to reality TV shows. I love them all. I think this is because I am a student of the human animal. I study people at work, the mall, gas stations, restaurants and everywhere else. I have a hard time keeping eye contact with whomever I am with in public places because I am always watching. Yes, I am the rude guy that stares. People are just as fascinating to me as they are irritating.

My favorite reality show is the granddaddy of them all, *Survivor*. If this show does not give us a perfect example of the human race, I don't know what does. Where else can we see friendships developed, alliances formed, and castaways making promises and last-minute betrayals at Tribal Council? I love to see who, at Tribal Council, pulls the knife out in the end only to plunge it into the back of the very friend to whom they swore an allegiance.

I also love seeing who can outwit, outlast and outplay the other castaways. The whole show makes for the perfect drama. I threaten to apply for the show every season and I think that I would survive. I have a healthy fantasy life. At the end of every episode, a tribe member is voted off.

No matter how much I love or hate that person, I always feel bad for them because they have to talk into the camera and say how they feel about getting the boot. Most people try to be nice and say that they had a wonderful experience and, "Hee-hee! I didn't see that coming! They got me!" I don't think I would be so gracious.

I was voted off the "island." The tribe had spoken, my torch was snuffed out, and I was sent away. What would I say to the camera? This has me laughing as I write this because of all the things I should not say. However, I would say something like this:

"This has been an amazing experience that I will never forget. I never thought in a million years that I would be blindsided like this. I know you did what you thought was best for the tribe. One individual is not as important as the whole tribe, now is it? You guys got me, and I wish you all well. Thanks for all the good times... Thanks for all the broken promises, abandonment and betrayal... it was awesome. I could have used a little help with this, but I guess I am on my own. I hope I make it. I hope Anna does not become even more suicidal. I hope my kids come out of this without too much damage. Hey, I will be thinking about you all as I pick up the broken pieces of my life. I will not forget you because you will be all I will be able to think about for the next decade. So long, and thanks again... for everything."

That just might get good ratings, don't you think?

We were off to survive on our own. I decided to give it a go ministry-wise, and if we should find a church that would take us, we would never tell them about what had happened. We went into survivor mode, and looking back, we didn't use the best judgment. We just needed to do something, anything that would restore us to some sense of stability. It was fight or flight for us, and we chose flight.

Barry, a friend of mine in San Diego, had just started a ministry to train up leaders. He invited me to come alongside and help. Anna and I thought this would be a great idea, and we decided to go for it. San

Diego was home, and going home sounded like the thing to do. The ministry was just getting off the ground, and that meant I didn't have a salary. I had to raise my own support. We had no place to live and no way of paying rent. In June 1997, we did what any logical person would do. We went to San Diego without a pot to pee in or a window to throw it out of. We just wanted to move on and I just wanted out of there. I wanted to get as far away from those people as I could. We packed our house, loaded the moving van, stuffed five of us in the car, and ran away to San Diego.

We put all our belongings in storage and moved in with Barry and his wife, Barb. Oh, did I mention that they were a family of five as well? Yeah, ten people in one house. It was crazy, but we managed. We enrolled the kids in school and started our new life. I did ministry stuff with Barry. Anna did Mom stuff. I also started a sales job to help bring in a little income. This didn't last very long. We had fled reality, and it wasn't long before we all realized that working in a ministry where I had to raise my own support was a bad idea. I was not very good at fund-raising. I started sending résumés to churches all over the United States.

Living with Barry and Barb lasted two or three months – I don't remember exactly, but it had come to an end. It was supposed to be temporary, and if I had no income, we could not get our own place. We got creative and stayed with different people, including family, and even went to Christian camps where they would put up pastors for free. Finally, we landed with some friends whom Anna had known for years, and I got a job driving buses for San Diego County. The pay was poor, but it was better than nothing. During this time, my son had his tonsils removed, and my oldest daughter broke her leg while I was speaking at a camp. To top it off, certain members of my extended family and I got into a huge fight. The details are not that important, but because of pride and prejudice, we didn't speak for several months.

I was stressed. I was emotionally drained, and no church that I had sent a résumé to was even calling me. I was a youth pastor with ten years of experience and no one called. I sent something like thirty résumés all over the U.S. and not even a nibble. I was getting angrier and more depressed by the week. One morning Anna asked me, "What are you going to do, Rudy?" Truth be known, I had no clue. The question ticked me off. I turned to her as I was walking out the door and said, "Drive a freaking bus and make the best out of it. What are you going to do?"

I walked out the door to go to my newfound career driving a bus, feeling stressed and disillusioned and wondering why no one wanted to hire me as their youth pastor.

CHAPTER 8

Critical Mass Confusion

In December 1997, just as the darkness of hopelessness and fear had settled in, the light broke through and someone called! A church in the Oregon area was interested in interviewing us. Anna called me at work, and I was elated. Finally, we could get back to normal! I called the senior pastor that afternoon, and after a thirty-minute phone call, we were being flown to Oregon for an interview.

We flew into the airport and were greeted by the pastor of the Northwest Church. We were treated well and were put up in a cozy bed-and-breakfast for the weekend visit. This was a well-needed vacation, complete with a little expense account for meals and a church van to drive. The first night we met the entire church staff. We all hit it off pretty well, and it looked like it could be a good fit.

The next day was the official interview with the board, and later that night we were offered the youth pastor position. A week and a half later, we loaded up again and were on the road, moving from San Diego to Oregon.

The Pacific Northwest is beautiful, with its 100-foot fir trees and mountains. Temperatures are rarely higher than seventy-eight degrees in the summer and it snows just enough in the winter to enjoy it, then it goes away about the time you are sick of it. It was a wonderful change of pace, and we loved it.

The church had found a house for us to rent, so the move was practically automatic. It took no time at all before we were settled in. There were a handful of kids in the youth group, and it was my job to go get the teenagers and get them involved. This was an easy task for me. I have always loved teenagers. In about a month, the youth ministry attendance nearly tripled. We started out with about fifteen to twenty kids, and a month later, we had close to sixty. A few months after that, we were in the eighties to nineties.

It was incredible how quickly we built relationships with the kids in the youth group. It was like we had been there forever. We had an absolutely wonderful time there. For me, things were as close to perfect as they could be. I was in my element, and it was oh so good. Anna's doctors had prescribed Prozac, and she was adjusting to the medication beautifully. She was doing very well, and it seemed like we had seen the worst of it. Good things were happening, and it felt good.

One of the good things was making new friends. Two of those friends were the music director, Curt, and his wife, Dona.

Our friendship had a little bit of a stressful beginning. I don't remember if it was me or someone else that made comment about people in the Northwest being a little thin-skinned and that there are a lot of people who get their feelings hurt easily. Dona, of course, had something to say about this. She said something about the emotional "crazies" she knew, and that she believed the city needed to put Prozac in the water for all the crazy people. She was trying to be funny, and it would have been… if Anna hadn't been taking Prozac.

To say that the situation was awkward is an understatement. With this glorious history between us at such an early point, you might think that we could never become friends. However, we did. We became great friends. Curt is a fun guy, and we had some of the best times together. Like the time he talked me into highlighting my hair, and he and Anna were the hairdressers. In the end, I had a bad hair color with white eyebrows. I looked like I was a cast member in *CATS*. More than all the hilarious and fun experiences, it was just good to have friends that loved us and knew how to be good friends. In time, he and Dona came to know our whole story and they never judged, never looked at us differently. Curt and Dona are probably two of the most genuine people I have ever met. They are the real deal. They have had their fair share of difficulty and have managed to keep their spirituality intact. What impresses me about them to this day is that they never sacrificed their humanity to their spirituality. They know who they are and who they are not. I appreciate them immensely.

Oregon was good times. Good people, good friends, good ministry. We left the ugly, bad experiences behind us, and tried to move on. It was a good place to start over and forget about the past. That would have been the thing to do, but I still hung on to what had happened back in California at First Church. I still thought about what had happened. I still wondered why Pastor Rich had lied to me, betrayed me and ignored me. I was having an awesome "now," and yet I was consumed by the past. The bitterness was a slow boil. The next set of events only made things worse.

Everything was going great, so this could only get better, right? Nope, we left one dysfunctional situation and walked right into an even more dysfunctional situation. It took a little time, but I started to figure out that there were some real issues with the pastor at the Northwest Church. He didn't lead to serve the people of the church, he set up scenarios that promoted himself and his sideline agendas. He was not exactly what I would have called an effective leader.

I started to separate myself from him as much as I could. I did not enjoy his company. I did not like his sense of humor. I did not like his self-centered, self-seeking agenda. More than anything else, I did not respect him.

After I had been there for a short time, he and I got into a very heated discussion. He was the denomination's regional representative, and our yearly state-wide meeting was taking place in Portland. The whole pastoral staff was supposed to attend. I felt like this was a place for him to parade us all over so everyone could see what a large team he led. Well, I wasn't going to be associated with this and told him that I would not be going. He decided to confront me about this in the parking lot on my way out. I had a migraine that day and was going home to rest. He thought that this was a good time to bring this situation up. If he had really understood me, he would not have taken his life into his own hands like this. He lived… and learned. I could not believe his lack of respect for my migraine. He walked up to me and said, "So, you think you are not going to the regional meeting?"

"No, I'm not," I said. "I have too many other things to do and it's not good for my family at this time. We have three small kids."

"I really think you should. It's important. I'll find someone to watch your kids."

"I appreciate that, but I am not going." At this point I was about to throw up because of the migraine.

"Look, I'm your elder and your pastor," he said. "You need to go and I expect you to go."

"*I am not going!* I just told you that it is not good for my family to be gone for a weekend. So, no, I'm not going!" I could feel the bile building up, and I decided that if I puked it was going to be on him.

"So that's it then? You're not going?"

"No *sir*, I am not!" (The "sir" was sarcastic, if you didn't catch that.)

In every other case in my life, if a pastor/boss was to ask me to do something, I would have done it. I am not someone who just says "no" to say "no." I did not respect him.

By this time, I knew I could get away with just about anything. He made his big stand and caved in at the end of his big confrontation, only to walk away practically pouting. I was beginning to develop and embrace a protective cocoon around myself. I had been hurt once and no one was going to do it again.

Let's face it – whether I respected the man or not, he was the boss and I was totally rude, disrespectful and insubordinate. He should have called me on it. He didn't even mention it again. I won. I won the battle and he lost, and it felt good! I protected myself, and even though I was a big jerk, I got what I wanted and I loved it! My character was slowly beginning to erode and I was becoming a man with a chip on my shoulder.

The Pacific Northwest experience continued to get worse by the day. Finally the news came out that the pastor's wife was addicted to methamphetamines, as well as had an affair and moved in with her newfound love. The pastor attempted to cover it up, but it exploded into a scandalous, stressful, confusing and painful mess.

While this was happening, in the background, something new was developing. Curt's in-laws, who were pastors in the south, came to town for a visit. Anna and I were able to meet with them on several occasions, and having been pastors for many years, they had a lot of wisdom to share about our current situation. It was refreshing to hear from them. I liked them a lot.

Pastor Jay and his wife were your typical, old-school Pentecostal-type people. They knew what they believed about God, politics and themselves. They did not waver on doctrinal issues, but they also genuinely loved people. Pastor Jay was a thick-framed, gray-haired, steely-eyed powerhouse. He could tell countless colorful stories and he made me laugh constantly. He was never afraid to say exactly what he thought, even if it hurt someone's feelings. It wasn't that he wanted to hurt anyone's feelings, he just told the truth. He liked to call it "shooting straight," and he shot straight a lot.

His wife was a short, gentle-spirited woman. She was very much the opposite personality of her husband. Her eyes were always loving and kind. When she spoke, people listened because of the sweetness in her voice and the impact of her wisdom. When Pastor Jay spoke, one listened because there was no choice involved. The contrast between the pastor of the Northwest Church and Pastor Jay was staggering. Pastor Jay just being there and talking to me helped to show me that I was in a go-nowhere, dead-end situation. I was in a desperate place and I knew it. He knew it, and he tried to help me understand it. I again felt hopeless. I began to feel the darkness and anger settle in. It seemed like an outside element was controlling my life, and I could do nothing but just stand there with my hands in my pockets and watch. Even with people all around me, I felt alone.

Anger was building and I wasn't sure how long I could control myself. I thought constantly about Pastor Rich. My thoughts were darting back and forth to California and what was happening in Oregon. The stress of what had happened in my life was catching me, strangling me. I had reached critical mass confusion and I wanted to run, but had no place to go.

With this lurking overhead, Anna and I made the best out of our circumstances. I secretly started sending résumés to churches and calling friends. I didn't really want to leave, but I was so tired of the Northwest Church that I just wanted out. We had only been there eight months! I was connecting with the kids in the youth group, but not like I thought I should – mostly because I couldn't stop thinking about the youth group I had left behind. I needed to make a decision, but I wasn't sure what to do. That is, until I bumped into Pastor Jay at a Little League game.

Pastor Jay was in town again, and there he was, watching his grandson's game directly across from the field where my son was playing. Pastor Jay walked over to say hi and ask us how things were. We updated him on our situation and he decided to give us some fatherly advice, which we gladly accepted. The conversation ended with an invitation to come to his church in the south.

CHAPTER 9

"Kentucky Fried Life"

The south was a new and exciting place, and provided a new lifestyle to adjust to. The surrounding beauty of the state was breathtaking. We had four seasons, which is something that a native San Diegan knows nothing about. I saw my first red tree in the fall and I practically wrecked my car looking at this new and strange phenomenon.

Our first month there, we experienced a little bit of culture shock. People there are nice. They greet you on the street and wave at every car they pass on the road whether they know the person driving or not. It was like living in the Land of Oz and all the southerners were munchkins. The niceness was overwhelming and the pace was, frankly, quite irritating.

With all of the hang-ups and bitterness that I was dealing with, adjusting to a new culture and environment was very difficult for me. Because I was broken and hurt, I dealt with every person and situation from a wounded place.

Southern people are some of the most generous and lovely people God ever created. They are good folks with warm hearts and open arms. They are people who want to help, with no ulterior motives. They are people who will freely interject themselves into a person's life. They want to know your story and all the details. I was not going to let that happen.

Pastor Jay was a good pastor, but he was what we can call "old school." It didn't take long for us to start butting heads, first a little, and then a lot. He had some expectations that were impossible to meet. His "in-your-face," "my-way-or-the-high-way" attitude and my newly formed "up-yours" attitude didn't mix well. It didn't matter what I did anyway; I could do no right. If I planned camp, it was too expensive or the place I was going was stupid. If I spoke on Sunday, I was too long or my points were watered down. I was berated constantly. The church had an outreach event on Halloween that I created and headed up. I had some talented volunteers, and together we pulled off a huge carnival-type event. In a community of 30,000, we had something like 10,000 attend. It was incredible. Pastor Jay told me that the reason I did so well at this event was because I had a "need to be seen." I got to the point where I finally ignored anything he said to me.

In the middle of all this, I was still trying to protect Anna from things that didn't even exist. I about drove myself crazy trying to shield her from people's attitudes and what they were saying, but she was doing great. She was being a mother and wife, plus she ran the food cupboard at church. She shopped for it, maintained it and handed out food to the less fortunate in the community every week. She had adjusted perfectly to her medication, and it looked as if all the depression and hopelessness was over.

I had nothing to worry about, and still I was scared to death that she would relapse. I caught myself building scenarios about bad things that were going to happen. I was constantly worried about her. I was now also practically obsessed with what had happened in California. At times I would get so angry at the pastor there that I was fantasizing about hurting him, beating him, choking him and punching him. There was a beast within that was changing me.

I wanted to go back to First Church. I wanted to go back to the way it was. I wanted my youth group, church and life back. Reality hit me during a conversation I had with Curt about it. He just looked at me and said, "You are not going back! You are just not going back!"

I realized then that I could never and would never go back. It did not help me to forgive or forget. I just came to my senses and I had to move on. It was a dark and sad realization for me. I truly wanted to go back. Not just go back to a place, but to another place in time and try to make it something else. The reality was that I could not, and now I was living this "Kentucky Fried life" and I hated it!

We had a lot of great times in the south. We met wonderful people and it was not a bad place to live, but we struggled financially and that put a huge damper on the experience. I started out working in retail, but things didn't work out and I quit. Anna and I became school bus drivers, and I took a paper route in which I delivered newspapers to about 100 homes in a very rural part of the south. From midnight to 5 a.m., I drove nothing but dirt roads and delivered newspapers to chicken ranches and homes in the netherworld. From 5 a.m. to 8 a.m., I drove a school bus. Our income was small, but luckily, the church paid the rent. We ate a lot of pancakes and peanut butter. Now, don't get the wrong idea here; we chose to do this and to live there. No one forced us to. The one time I mentioned that I was having a hard time financially, Pastor Jay chewed me out for being ungrateful and told me that I had a better deal than anyone on the church staff. So we just plugged along.

One thing that tilted our world forever was when Pastor Jay convinced Anna that she needed to stop taking her medication and let

God move in her life. This was really bad advice. It is never a good idea to mess with medication that is working for someone who has psychological problems. As far as I was concerned, God had already intervened and she was fine.

When Anna didn't stop taking the medication, Pastor Jay put pressure on her to get off her medication and have faith in God. Finally, she gave in, went to a doctor and slowly weaned off the Prozac. I don't know why I went along with this.

We moved to the south in July of 1998, and by December 1999, we knew that it wasn't for us. There were several reasons we had to leave. I was so consumed by my own anger and pain that I no longer had the heart to deal with some of the people in the church.

Pastor Jay was a very difficult man to work for. I loved him, he was overall a good guy, but I could not do what he expected. It came to the point where it was almost a junior-high game of "he said, she said."

For example, during Christmas, I had raised some money to buy new clothes for some of the less fortunate kids in our youth program. I called the lady in charge of the church finances to get the money so we could do our shopping trip the next day with the kids. This simple request started an interrogation, which led to a horrible argument. I really didn't know why she was being so evasive about giving me the funds. I had an event scheduled to take six teenagers shopping and I needed the money. The conversation ended with her threatening to tell Pastor Jay, which she did. Pastor Jay took her side. Once again, he chastised and berated me for being selfish, overbearing and rude. I finally did get to take them on their shopping trip with the money we had raised, which was all I had wanted to do in the first place.

I later learned that Pastor Jay had told the lady that I could not be trusted with money. I called Curt and Dona and told them what had happened, and Dona leveled with me. She said, "You can't win here, Rudy. You need to just resign." Remember, Pastor Jay was her father, so I took that advice to heart. I quit that afternoon.

I submitted my letter of resignation the week after Christmas of 1999. We didn't actually leave until February, 2000. I sent résumés to churches all over the place again. I interviewed in California and Texas. Each place seemed hopeful, but they went with other people. I decided to go back to San Diego and go back to work as a pipefitter in the shipyards, which was my former line of work.

My relationship with Pastor Jay was horribly strained. My last week there, I had lunch with him. He used this time to tell me exactly how he felt about me. He told me that I was leaving him holding the bag. His comments were hurtful and mean-spirited. There was no point for me to say anything. I just ate my lunch and listened. I loved the way he brought up my wife's issues. He knew about her depression and what had happened in California. He basically told me how crazy she was and that I was even crazier.

This was interesting to me for two reasons. Firstly, he was the one who had convinced my wife to get off her medication, and secondly, he was the one who put pressure on her when she did not. He told us that if she continued to take the prescribed medication that it would block God from performing a miracle in her life, and that she would never be healed from her mental issues. Then he felt the need to bring up her issues and hang-ups at our last meeting together.

When he invited us to move across country he told us "if you have one more bad experience in church, you would be out of ministry." He was correct. That was my last bad experience in ministry. Shortly, I would leave the ministry for good.

CHAPTER 10

The Big Three

There are probably no perfect places on planet Earth, but San Diego comes close. I think that this is where God goes on vacation. Moving back to San Diego was going home. It was the place Anna and I both grew up. It was where we got married and it was where all of our friends and family were.

My sister was an apartment manager and made sure we had a place to live once we arrived. We pulled into the parking lot and everyone was there. My kids were greeted by their aunt and uncle and their grandma and grandpa. I was happy to see my children reunite with their family.

I got my old job back as a pipefitter in the shipyards and I was right back where it all started. I had been working there when First Church hired me. It was the place I had desperately wanted to leave to go into full-time ministry, and here I was again. This time, I liked it. There were no lying, crazy egomaniacs here, just a bunch of guys earning a living and getting along. I was reunited with what seemed like thousands of old friends. It looked like everyone was still there, and it took about an hour for me to readjust. It was as if I had never been apart from these guys. I was a "yard-bird" again. ("Yard-bird" is a Navy term for a civilian worker.)

I have held many different jobs in my life. My résumé has the work experience of five people, at least. I have been a stock-room clerk, sales-floor clerk, cashier, service-desk clerk and undercover store-detective, and this was all at K-Mart! I have worked as a painter, a city bus driver, a school bus driver, a newspaper carrier, a pipefitter, a quality-assurance inspector, superintendent and pastor, all by the time I was forty! The longest and most memorable job I held was fitting pipe.

I started fitting pipe in 1984. My dad was a pipefitter, and so naturally, I wanted to be a pipefitter… right? Not exactly, and it wasn't my father's dream for me to be a pipefitter either. He and my Mom wanted me to go to college and become… well, anything as long as I had a college degree. I did no such thing. I graduated from high school and started attending community college while working at a clothing store as the stock boy. Long story short, I bombed out of college and my dad got me a job in the shipyards of San Diego as a pipefitter helper. Don't misunderstand me here. He didn't really offer me the job. He just told me to show up on Monday and start working.

Now, my dad has a way with words and he has a way with life. To him, if I wasn't going to get a college degree, then I was still going to be a productive member of society. Therefore, I was going to become a pipefitter, or else! I wasn't sure what "or else" meant, but I figured I had better not find out. So, guess where I was the following Monday? I was sitting in his truck at 4 a.m., going to work, that's where! I think he was trying to scare me and it almost worked. He was the foreman and he made sure that I was working in the fuel tanks my first day on the job. They were deep, rusty, nasty and smelly fuel tanks. It was a dirty, sweaty job with tight spots and heavy lifting, but I loved it. I loved the paycheck, too! This is where Dad's scare tactic went awry. I made more money in a week than I made in a month as a stock boy. I think I also loved it because I loved the guys.

The people in the shipyards are a great bunch of human beings and they are far from perfect. Among these people, whom to this day I will always call my friends, are drug-addicts, crack-heads, alcoholics, gang-bangers, bikers, rednecks, fascists, felons, murderers, dealers, bank-robbers, perverts, and every sort of deviant you can imagine. There are also retired Navy enlisted men and officers all over the place as well. There are even a couple of pastors running around, and just your average run-of-the-mill guys. The one thing that these people have is respect – a genuine respect for their fellow worker, and if someone is in trouble, these guys rally.

If someone dies, they take a collection. If someone has a baby, they take a collection. If someone moves, people help. (Not me, though. I hate moving. I've moved fifteen times in twenty years. I get a free pass.) I think what I love about them all is that they all have what I call the "Popeye principle." Popeye always said, "*I am what I am and that's all I am…*" and these guys are who they are and that's it. If you don't like the way they are, you will more than likely receive a very heartfelt derogatory hand gesture! Yes – I know, rude and hateful, but it's a shipyard thing.

I liked the idea of being just a regular guy, a working-class stiff with a family to feed. No one expected anything from me except to show up on time, do my job and go home. Yes, it was really good to be back.

At first, I was going to work in the shipyards until something in ministry became available. I sent résumés to churches for about three months, but I was so tired and burned out on the church scene that I gave up. Yet, before we knew it, we were youth pastors at a small church in a town called Lemon Grove, where my good friend Jim was the pastor. I met Jim in 1984. He had been in ministry for two weeks, working as the junior-high ministries director at the church I attended. We hit it off immediately and we spent the next several years working in ministry together. Naturally, we would go to his church.

They couldn't pay me much, but I didn't care. I was just fine being a part-time pastor and working full-time someplace else. This would actually be our second tour-of-duty at the Lemon Grove Church. I was a part-time youth pastor there before First Church hired me. We were coming full circle, and it was a little strange, but it was nice to be home with people I knew. No one there was pretentious or phony. Truth be known, the Lemon Grove Church was the only ministry experience of ours that did not end with some weird story. We were there, we served the people, they let us serve and love them, and they served and loved us back. I didn't really see it at the time, but this was a great church. It wasn't flashy with flashy people, but just a nice place to belong. Jim is a great pastor. There is not a pretentious fiber within him. He is the real deal. He also possesses the "Popeye principle." He is who he is – nothing more, nothing less.

We had arrived and I had the big three: Family and friends, and a good church. It was an awesome contrast with where I had been. The previous three years were like walking in a minefield wearing clown shoes that were too big. I had traveled from one bomb to another, and I was getting blown to hell mentally, emotionally and spiritually. By the time I got back to San Diego, I was bleeding and broken. I was a mess. The big three were able to apply a tourniquet and stop the bleeding for a while.

Family is always good to have in your corner. Most families, whether they are affluent or poor, stable or screwed up, will be there for you. My family had no idea of the magnitude of what had happened to me and that was because I hadn't told them. I felt a little overwhelmed about my "minefield" experience. I didn't like talking about it and I was also a little embarrassed.

No one understood why I was back and what I was doing or why I had taken a temporary leave from ministry, but they just let me be me, and I was good with that. They all tried to offer advice on something that I had really told them nothing about. They only knew bits and pieces. Because they didn't really know what was going on, they could not give any advice that made sense, and I wasn't really listening to them anyway. I wasn't in the mood for a loving family, genuinely concerned about me and my wife and kids, to give me advice. I didn't think I needed the advice, but they did offer the acceptance that I needed.

The shipyard friends, the yard-birds, were the people that gave me respect, but that also taught me respect. What they taught me was that giving respect and honor was not about a person's position in life. It was about being a human being, an equal in life's voyage. These guys were better "Christians" than some of the pastors I had known.

The Lemon Grove Church and my family gave me acceptance, respect and love without pretense – just love. The last three experiences I'd had with best friends, mentors, pastors and churches for the most part, had managed to assassinate my hope. My family and friends, combined with the Lemon Grove Church, brought some temporary, but much needed healing. I felt okay. I did not feel normal, or like I was myself, I just felt good enough to survive.

I still thought about Pastor Rich and First Church every day. The Northwest Church and "Kentucky Fried" experiences still haunted me. I was losing ground, slipping into myself and getting dark and empty.

CHAPTER 11

Slip-sliding Away

It was May 2000 when Anna got that awful feeling of hopelessness again. Even the simplest of tasks overwhelmed her. She was slipping back into depression. I first noticed it in her personality. Things that usually excited her did not cause a reaction. Unresponsive was a good way to describe her. No smiling, no laughing, no crying and no anger. She was just flat.

I didn't have to say a word to her about it. Anna recognized her symptoms and made an appointment with the doctor immediately. She did not want to get to the point where she was unable to function. I didn't want her to end up back in a mental hospital. She was worried; I was scared. The psychologist prescribed Prozac once again and assured us that there was nothing to worry about. Anna would be back to herself in three to six weeks.

Six weeks came and went, and there wasn't much of a change in Anna. She was overwhelmed and tired most of the time. I was very worried about her. In fact, I was panicked. I feared she would fall into a deep depression and become suicidal. I was spinning in circles trying to prevent my wife from either going into the hospital or killing herself. I was overwhelmed, and the strange thing is that I didn't tell anyone how I felt. I was scared and alone, but I didn't have to be alone.

I suppose I didn't want to admit to being scared because if I did that, then I would have to face the fact that there really was something serious going on with Anna. I did what most would try to do. I tried to rescue her. I tried to fix it by telling her that she would feel better with just a little time. I would tell her to be strong and "tough it out," but that did not work for a second. I could not control the situation. I could not fix it. Anna was slipping, and the tighter I tried to hold her in place, the further she slid. I thought that if we could all just hold on until the Prozac started to take effect, we would make it, but the Prozac was not working.

We returned to the psychiatrist and reported Anna's lack of progress and she confirmed my biggest fear. The medication was not doing what it was supposed to do. I immediately began to reason with the doctor.

"The Prozac worked before, so shouldn't it be working now?"

"Sometimes, when a patient stops taking a med and tries to go back after a period of time, the medication no longer has an effect," the psychiatrist explained. "Chemically, the body no longer responds."

"So, what do we do now?" Anna asked.

The psychiatrist produced her prescription pad: "We try something else and see if that works. I am going to wean you off the Prozac and once you are done with that, you start taking Welbutrin."

This was the first step in Anna's quest for the right medication. Five doctors later and somewhere around twenty medications later, with every imaginable combination of those medications, Anna had compiled a very impressive list of chemicals flowing though her bloodstream.

The summer came and went. Anna and I did our best to keep things positive. By the fall, we were somewhat back on course. The kids were in regular school, Anna was an assistant apartment manager and I was working at my new job in ship repair. We were part-time youth pastors and other than Anna's battle with depression, our life seemed fine.

But life was far from being fine. Anna was struggling not to drown in depression and I was struggling every day to understand what my role was in this illness. Nothing I said or did mattered. It felt like Anna rejected all my efforts, but the truth is she wasn't rejecting me. It was the illness rejecting me. There is not a positive side to clinical depression. Depression will suck the life out of a person, as well as everyone around them. It is a stubborn beast that will destroy hope and everything of value in a family. Anna's depression seeped into my soul and drained me of my hope. I slowly began to lose my emotional footing and I was sliding myself.

I had my own issues I was not dealing with. My bitterness and anger were not helping. I was obsessed with Rich and what he had done. Yes, I was angry at the Northwest pastor and Pastor Jay, but even though they did play a part in why I was angry, nothing compared to Rich's outright betrayal.

My mind began to drift into unrealistic thinking. I wanted to call him at first and just give him a piece of my mind. I just wanted to tell him what a piece of crap I thought he was. I wanted to tell him what he had done. He abandoned me, and look at what was happening now! It was his fault! He always said to people going through a difficult situation, "How big is your God?" Well, how big was his? He could have seen us through this! He could have seen us through all of this. These thoughts constantly darted around my mind, day and night.

Soon the desire to call him left and I wanted a face-to-face encounter with him. I literally started to fantasize about driving to his office, walking in there and physically kicking the living hell out of him. I was getting more violent and dark by the day. I would find myself sitting alone, thinking about how I would do it. I would walk in happy and jovial. Then I'd strike and I would beat him unconscious. My heart would race and my breathing would get rapid every time I played the plan over in my mind. Then I'd regain some restraint and common sense and say to myself, "You can't do that." I'd talk myself out of doing something so ridiculous.

I had slipped from a bad place to a disturbing place. My disturbing mindset didn't end there, and it didn't stop for a very long time.

CHAPTER 12

The Fall

Usually in about the middle of September, I start feeling great anticipation for the coming of fall. Fall is my favorite time of year. I love the crispness of the air, the smell of pumpkin spices, the colors of the landscape. Fall brings in warm comfort foods and baked cookies, and it marks the beginning of football season. The fall of 2000 was no exception. I couldn't wait for the season to come, but this year would not be filled with chocolate cookies and cider.

The first thing that made this fall less festive was a decision that I made. Sitting in church one Sunday morning, I decided to leave the ministry. I was sitting there watching the people at the Lemon Grove Church singing songs. I listened to them and watched their faces. Everyone looked so happy. What were they so happy about? I was not happy. I was tired. I felt angry at them for being content with their lives. That is when I came to some serious realizations about myself.

I was tired of church, tired of people, and tired of broken promises. I was tired of my wife being sick and I was tired of being alone. I was tired of the ministry and I was tired of pretending that I was okay. I was tired of putting on a smile and listening to these people and their struggles and needs. I had nothing left to give. I had lost the desire to give them anything. I was not the same.

I had become a pathetic shell of what I once was. I did not wake up one morning and choose for my life to be turned upside down, but it was. I did not intend to change, but I did. Later that week, I called Pastor Jim at the Lemon Grove Church and invited him to coffee. As we sat at Starbucks and enjoyed coffee together, I resigned as youth pastor. Jim graciously allowed me to bow out and we departed as friends. I gave Jim some lame excuse about needing more time at work. I don't remember exactly what I said, but it was not the truth. I just didn't have the energy to be real and tell the truth. The truth was I was sick of church, sick of church people and sick of ministry. I was done.

My minister's credential renewal forms came in the mail about this time. I promptly deposited them in the nearest garbage. My life as a minister was over. I vowed that I would never be in ministry again. This proclamation made Anna sad, and I think it made people who cared about me sad too. I didn't care what anyone thought. My mind was made up. The bitterness had won.

In October, Anna took the final turn for the worse. This time was not like the other times. She was getting horribly depressed and distant. I could tell that she was trying to pretend that everything was normal. I could see her fighting the darkness, but in the end, the last bit of life left in her was flickering out. There were trips to the doctor, who prescribed additional medications.

Two days after Thanksgiving, Anna was admitted to a behavioral health facility. She was too depressed to function, and despite my efforts to prevent them, the thoughts of suicide came. Anna was no longer safe. She had become a danger to herself. The illness had won.

CHAPTER 13

Funny Farm 101

(An introduction to the mental health facility)

ICU

The ICU, or Intensive Care Unit, is where the journey begins for the patients, and it's the place that no patient wants to revisit. As nice as the doctors and nurses try to make it, it is filled with unpleasantness. Granted, it's designed for the patient's safety and protection, but the patient views the ICU as hell. Anna was no exception. She hated it. Here's why.

The ICU is the first stop for anyone entering the hospital, no matter how severe or minor the diagnosis. A person that may be marginally depressed could very well be interacting with a person who is schizophrenic. I always wondered why the suicidal were allowed to mingle with the homicidal. It didn't seem like a good mix at all!

All walks of life are in the ICU: The homeless, the wealthy, thugs, blue-collar, white-collar, black, white and in-between. This is where the journey starts for everyone – no exceptions.

There are few freedoms in ICU, and by few, I mean none. The day will be completely scheduled for you:

- 6:00 – 6:30 a.m. – Shower time
- 7:00 a.m. – Breakfast

- 8:15 a.m. – Group therapy
- Noon – Lunch
- 1:00 p.m. – Therapy
- 2:30 – 3:30 p.m. – Nap time
- 3:30 – 4:30 p.m. – Recap of the day (New staff; shift change)
- 5:00 p.m. – Dinner
- 7:00 p.m. – Visiting hour
- 8:00 p.m. – Evening session
- 10:00 p.m. – Lights out

There are three areas in the ICU where patients are allowed to be:

- The Common Room: This is where all group therapy sessions are held, meals are served and it's where the television and pay phones are. These are only allowed to be used during the free time.
- The Outside Recreation/Designated Smoking Area: It is really quite nice if you can get used to the high fences and barbed wire. Actually, it is not barbed wire, it is a thick, green mesh that is angled in a manner that makes it impossible to climb over. There is a basketball court, a ping-pong table and picnic-style benches. (There really isn't anything more entertaining than a game of three-on-three basketball or a heated ping-pong match where the players are all hopped up on mood-stabilizers and Thorazine. There are very few arguments and very few points scored!)
- The Sleeping Area: This is usually a room that is shared between two or more patients and where you keep your clothing and your personal items. If you are on suicide watch, you get to sleep next to a large window so the nurses can keep an eye on you. This room is known as the fishbowl. Privacy is not an option. You are watched constantly.

The thing that Anna hated most was that you are constantly told, "You can't." You can't have certain personal products like hairspray or hair gel with alcohol in them. You can't have anything sharp like pencils, pens, hair clips or jewelry. You can't have certain clothing like sweats with strings in the waistband or shoelaces in your shoes. In other words, you can have nothing that can choke you or anyone else. You may receive gifts from your visitors, but you can't have them until the nurse at the nurse's station has approved the items.

Food items brought to you must be in the original package. You can't receive a visitor unless allowed by your doctor. You can't receive phone calls unless approved, nor can you make phone calls without permission. Depending upon your status, you can't even go to the bathroom or take a shower by yourself. A nurse has to watch and make sure you are not doing something that could potentially cause harm.

The ICU is designed for the safety and well-being of the patient. It has to have rigid policies in place because of the diversity of people and their diagnoses. That in no way means that the people there like it.

Visiting Hour

I hated to visit when Anna was in the ICU. It scared me. You might think, "Aw, c'mon Rudy, what was so scary?" The people! The people in there are scary. Anna would give me the rundown when I was in there. She would point out the suicidal, homicidal and psychotic. There were descriptions like, "That guy put three cops in the hospital just trying to get him here," and, "She hears voices that tell her to do weird things... like kill herself... and other people." See? There was scary stuff in there!

I asked Anna if she was scared. "No," she said. "I just keep to myself and they leave me alone. Besides, I'm suicidal, so the homicidal maniacs can't scare me." I had no reply.

I was privileged with the opportunity not only to see people in the ICU, I got to experience them. These people from every walk of life and tax bracket were at their lowest possible point in life. They were branded as "crazy" and "unfit" by society, family and friends. I was scared of some of them, but I felt their confusion and pain.

The worst part of visiting ICU was not the scary people, though. It was the sad people. People who were at rock bottom, people who were lonely and no one came to visit them. My observation showed me hopeless and depressed people making their last effort to survive. When family and friends don't show, it only confirms their fears that they are worthless and will never find the hope they so desperately need.

I remember in particular, a lady about forty years old, waiting for her husband and daughter to come and see her. She would sit in the closest chair by the door, waiting. Visiting time is only an hour in ICU, and she sat there the entire hour every night. No one ever came. I made sure I went to see Anna as often as I could. It was difficult going every day, but on the days I couldn't, I'd call during visiting hour so Anna would not be in the same situation as that woman.

The East Wing

Once the patients have spent time in ICU and are no longer considered a danger to themselves or others, they can graduate to the East Wing. This is where those who still can't quite face life and have other needs go for help. Those needs can be anything from self-cutting and self-abuse to eating disorders, drug addiction, hearing voices and dissociation. The neediest ones by far were those being treated for some form of severe depressive disorder. I can tell you that business at the hospital is never slow. It's the basic rule of supply and demand.

Depressive disorders affect approximately 18.8 million American adults, or about 9.5% of the U.S. population, age eighteen or older in a given year. This includes severe depressive disorder, dysthymic disorder and bipolar disorder. Given that, it's safe to say that the majority of the people admitted to a mental health facility are depressed or that depression is a part of their diagnosis.

Now, just to make it easy, let's call it one in ten people in the United States have some form of depression. Now, think about the different groups of people in this world you are associated with – work, church, PTA, the softball league, the Shriners, etc. If your company has 800 employees, eighty of them are possibly depressed. The population of Las Vegas, where I lived while writing this, is about 1,375,765 people. I am more than likely correct in estimating that nearly 130,000 people in Las Vegas are suffering from some form of depression. Depression is everywhere, and places like the East Wing specialized in helping people manage their illness. Any mental health professional's goal is to see the patient go home and tackle life again. This is sometimes easier said than done. Many men and women return several times, but the goal never changes.

Anna made it out of the ICU in about four days and transferred to the East Wing. The days in the East Wing are structured too, just not as rigidly as ICU. Every day starts with the same question: "On a scale from one to ten, how are you feeling today?" Every nurse, therapist, psychologist and psychiatrist asks the same question. If the number is lower than five that means that you really need to be there. If the number is higher, there is progress. When Anna arrived, she was hovering around a two to three, which meant that in the professionals' opinions, she needed to be admitted to the "Funny Farm" once again.

CHAPTER 14

Hotdogs, Happy Meals and Hamsters

I was no better prepared for Anna's second visit to the hospital than I was for the first. I think that deep down I knew all along that she would end up in the hospital again, but I was hoping that it would turn out differently and she would feel better. Looking back, I wish I had prepared myself for what was going to happen. I knew that I was going to have to step up, take over and be daddy-mommy again. I knew what was going to happen, but still, I was somewhat blindsided, not by her hospitalization, but by my lack of preparation.

I found myself sitting in my living room explaining to my children what was going on with Mommy and why she was in the hospital. This was not an easy task. My kids do not take anyone's word at face value. When I told them, "Mommy is in the hospital because her emotions are sick and she doesn't feel happy," I got looks that said, "You have got to be kidding me, Dad."

They were not buying my safe little storybook explanation. The conversation went a little like this:

Me: "...So that's why Mommy is in the hospital."

Aaron, age eight: "So, she isn't happy and she is in the hospital?"

Me: "Well, yeah, you know, her emotions are sick."

Breanna, age ten: "Why does she have to be in the hospital? What are they going to do there that can't be done here? We are not there and that is going to make her sadder."

Me: "Yes, but it's better for her to be there so the doctors can help her get over feeling so sad."

Rebekah, age six: "I'm sad, too. Can I go with Mommy?"

Me: "No, that is a grown-up place."

Aaron: "What is she unhappy about?"

Me: "Uh… well, things." (Yes… I get stupider the longer the conversation goes on.)

Breanna: "Things? What things?"

Me: "Uhhhhhhh…"

Aaron: "It makes no sense."

Me: "Well, it's safer for her there."

All three: "Safe from what?"

That's when the conversation started to circle the drain. I messed up when I said "things." I should have never said that. Now, how was I supposed to explain to them that their mother was suicidal and needed a safe environment in order to assure her survival? Three kids looked at me for answers and I had nothing. I didn't know what to say or how to get out of it. Then Rebekah said something that bailed me out:

"Can I have a hamster?"

Holy change of subject, Batman! I was saved!

"A hamster… well, we need to talk about that," I said, relieved. "Let's talk about it on the way to Mickey D's." I was off the hook. Hamsters and Happy Meals saved my neck.

Thank God that my sister lived right around the corner. The first time Anna was in the hospital, I had a church family to help with the kids. I worked at the church and Breanna went to the elementary school there. The other two stayed with a sitter, a good friend who never asked for a penny. This time I was working in the shipyards and I started at 6 a.m. All three of them were in school now, and school didn't start until 9:30. Without my sister being right there, I would have imploded.

This is how it worked. At 4 a.m., I got up and got showered and dressed for work. I collected backpacks, made lunches and put everything by the door. We picked out school clothes and put them inside the backpacks the night before so no one had to go to school naked. Then I made my lunch. At 4:30 a.m., I got everyone else up and they stumbled around in pajamas in utter bewilderment. At exactly 4:45, I gave the order to go to the car and everyone grabbed their lunches and backpacks and piled into the car. I drove for three minutes and we all piled out and staggered to my sister's apartment. I dropped the kids off and I went to work.

My sister got them up for school, got them dressed, combed hair and drove them to school, as well as picked them up in the afternoon. I habitually forgot something; homework, socks, lunches, or even their school clothes. It didn't take long before I just gave my sister a key to my place so she could go and retrieve whatever item I might forget on any given day.

I would pick everyone up after work and go home for the evening. At first, it was nice. I'd come home, make sure that homework was done and make dinner. We would do laundry together and then do the nightly ritual of baths and television. It didn't take long before we were all tired and things got sloppy. I mean really sloppy.

Laundry piled up and so did dinner dishes. I tried to build an environment of teamwork, but that didn't work out very well. I was too burned-out to enforce the rules and I let things slide. We merely survived. I tried to let the kids be kids, but I failed many times. Looking back on those days, I put way too much on them, and when things didn't get done, I lost my cool. I'd yell at them and make them do what they were expected to do. My sister finally had to call me and tell me to knock it off. I didn't appreciate the call at the time, but I listened and I cooled my jets. I later appreciated her stepping in. She knew what was really happening. I was stressed and upset because of Anna, and my kids were getting the fallout. It wasn't fair to them, and I will always be thankful that she did the right thing and stepped in and told me a thing or two.

Remember, I was angry about life in general anyway, so this could have escalated into a potentially abusive situation. Now eight years later, I still feel ashamed over some of the things I said and did during that time. Now, don't read into this. I didn't beat them or emotionally harm them. I was just harsh and impatient. I tried to apologize to them several times and they looked at me like I was sprouting a third eye. I guess I took it all harder than they did.

One night I was cooking dinner, and I was emotionally and physically exhausted. All I wanted to do was get dinner made and have a somewhat eventless evening. So, one by one, all three of my children came into the kitchen and complained about what I was making.

It was hot dogs and macaroni and cheese. The complaints were not that bad, but I was not in the mood. I heard first, "Oh, goody… hot dogs again?" from my sarcastic oldest daughter, Bree. Then about five minutes later, Aaron came in and looked around. "There is no ketchup, so this is gonna be gross." Rebekah came in next and looked in the pots, said, ""Yuck… I hate hot dogs," and stormed out of the kitchen.

I flung my spoon across the kitchen into the sink.

"You are going to eat what I give you… you… ungrateful bastards!" I said.

Aaron said, "Ungrateful what?"

"You heard me!"

"Oh, I am so telling Mom!" Bree said gleefully, as Bekah giggled.

Perhaps I should have been more concerned about hurting my children's feelings, but as it turned out, they didn't care one tiny bit that I called them a name. All they cared about was that they were going to get to tell on me, and that was pure gold to them. Dad was going to get it when Mom found out. To this day, they have not let me forget that. If I start a sentence with, "You are acting like…" they finish it, "Like what, dad… an ungrateful bastard?"

Oh, they did tell Anna that night when she called. Without any hesitation at all, Bree opened the conversation, "Hi Mom! Dad called us ungrateful bastards."

That is how it went down. Then each gave her an account of my transgression and smiled at me as they told her. I sat there, took my medicine and let each one watch me watch them tell on me. They didn't just like it, they were cherishing the moment! Yes, I got it; I got it good – once over the phone and once in person. I deserved it.

CHAPTER 15

Diagnosis— She's Crazy

Except for a brief day-trip home on Christmas day 2000, Anna resided at the hospital from the weekend after Thanksgiving until the following Easter. The decision of whether or not to let Anna go home was decided on a weekly basis. There were several things to be considered before letting her go home. I think the biggest reason she was not allowed to go home was because of the many different sides of her diagnosis.

When I first learned that Anna was not just suffering from severe depressive disorder; she was also bipolar, I was devastated. If there was one thing that I feared, it was that she was going to get a diagnosis that labeled her as a crazy person. This did exactly that in my mind. I was married to a crazy woman.

When Anna's doctor told me that she was bipolar, I looked at him and said, "Are you sure?" I can't quite describe the look he shot me as he answered my question. "Yes, I am sure." I didn't want to hear this news. I wanted Anna to have a little depression and to be able to come home soon. I thought that Anna would no longer be able to function in everyday society and that she was damaged beyond repair because she was bipolar. In layman's terms, I freaked out.

I was remembering every myth and horrible story I had ever heard about crazy people with bipolar disorder. Bipolar people were serial killers and heard voices that made them do unspeakable things. With the help of Anna's doctor and other mental health workers at the hospital, I was educated about the illness called bipolar disorder – formerly known as manic depression. I learned that bipolar disorder is an illness that can make a person's normal moods seem extreme because their mood can swing from very low (depression) to very high (mania).

Depression, of course, is when people feel very sad. Sometimes people have this feeling of sadness, and it can go on for a long period of time. People experiencing this may not want to get out of bed or even eat. They lose all interest and no longer enjoy things they used to do. Mania is the other side of bipolar disorder.

Mania may start with a happy feeling, like a "high." In some cases, mania has resulted in a person being very irritable and angry. People with mania do very outrageous and unpredictable things. I was at a support group for people who had spouses with bipolar disorder once, and I met people whose spouses spent their life savings and huge bonus checks on ridiculous things like junk bonds and baseball cards.

Anna's diagnosis was a little different. It was classified as bipolar II. This can best be described as the same as bipolar disorder, but without the mania. A bipolar II episode usually does not go to the full extremes of mania. This can make bipolar II more difficult to diagnose, since the "highs" or manic episodes may simply appear as a period of successful, high productivity.

I have learned to love the "hypomanic" episodes. A lot happens, things get cleaned and stuff gets done that I don't have to do. It may sound selfish for me to think like this, but I had to take the good with the bad. If Anna wants to clean out the entire garage, she is going to do it no matter what I say… so be it. Besides, getting in the way of a bipolar person who has her mind made up is like stepping in front of a slow-charging rhinoceros. You can see it coming, you know it is coming, but there isn't a whole lot you are going to do to stop it. It is best just to step aside and let it through.

Anna was now diagnosed as bipolar II, and let me tell you, it explained a lot. Years of mysteries were finally solved. I never could figure out why Anna would get annoyed and irritated over what I thought were ridiculous things, and then go on a spree of cleaning or organizing. One time she was disturbed by the stains on the side of the garbage cans. I didn't think much about it at all. She was serious about it. The next thing I knew, the garbage cans were in the driveway getting bleached and scrubbed down. That led to scrubbing the oil stains on the pavement, and then rearranging the garage and developing a whole new trash delivery system. I remember going out to the driveway as she was up to her elbows in a trash can full of suds.

I asked her, "What are you doing?"

"Cleaning these trash cans because I care and obviously you don't," she replied.

What does a guy say to that? Nothing, if he is smart.

Most people have seen the infomercials where they offer the consumer a product for $19.95 and then say the famous, "…But that's not all! For a limited time, you get two widgets for the price of one! And that's not all, call now and get blah blah…" I felt like I was experiencing the real-life infomercial offer from Anna's doctors. I didn't just get the bipolar disorder complete with severe depression and a lifetime supply of suicidal tendencies; I also got the new and improved psychological disorder, BPD – Borderline Personality Disorder! It was like hitting the psychiatrist diagnosis jackpot. What is Borderline Personality Disorder?

"Borderline Personality Disorder (BPD) is characterized by instability in moods, interpersonal relationships, self-image and behavior. This instability often disrupts family life and work life, and the individual's sense of self-identity. BPD is very common, affecting two percent of adults, mostly young women. Symptoms may include intense bouts of anger, depression and anxiety that may last only hours, or at most a day. These may be associated with episodes of impulsive aggression, self-injury and drug or alcohol abuse. Some view themselves as fundamentally bad or unworthy. People with BPD often have highly unstable patterns of social relationships. The fear of abandonment can be related to difficulty feeling emotionally connected to important persons when they are physically absent, leaving the individual feeling lost and perhaps worthless. Suicide threats and attempts may occur along with anger at perceived abandonment and disappointments" (National Institute of Mental Health).

So what did this all mean to me, the husband of the person with major depression, bipolar disorder and borderline personality disorder? It meant I was in trouble. I was in over my head and I had no way of knowing how to deal with any of this.

My first inclination was to run like hell. This would be a normal reaction since I was scared spitless. I don't know if a statistic exists, but spouses and significant others walk away from people with mental disorders quite often – especially those with BPD. I did not, so that meant I had to learn to deal with it. Eventually I did, but it was not an easy job.

CHAPTER 16

Half Dome; Half Doom

I decided not to walk away. It was not a very hard decision. My thought process was, "Why would I wuss out now?" At this stage in the game, it kind of reminded me of when I climbed Half Dome in Yosemite Valley nearly twenty years ago.

There were several of us, maybe fifteen, in our conglomeration of adventurers. We had a revelry call of 4:30 a.m. and it was up, get dressed and pack a lunch. This is not just a hike. It is more like a series of hikes rolled up into one huge, death defying journey. I will try my best to describe it.

There are no buses running that early in the morning in the valley, so we had no other choice but to walk or bribe someone else in the camp to get up and drive us there. Fat chance with our lot of lazy sleep-enthusiasts! The mile-and-a-half warm-up which led to the trailhead did nothing to prepare us for the uphill climb to the top of beautiful Vernal Falls.

Most people spend the day accomplishing this hike, but we were just getting started. Did I mention that this is all uphill? It is a nicely paved trail, complete with handrails, which is quite nice except for the uphill part. Once you get to the top, it changes from trail to rock-climbing in order to get to the top of the falls. It's exhilarating. For most people, this is quite a feat and normal people will end their travels here; but not us. We adventured for several more hours.

Next, we climbed Nevada Falls. It is rough because it is also all uphill. Then, we traipsed through Little Yosemite Valley and came to what seemed like 100 miles of switchback trails. These are back-and-forth trails that go on for miles up a steep incline. These switchbacks are a version of hell. It was so difficult that even at the age of twenty-four years old I thought I was going to die. Once we completed the switchback trail, we did more rock-climbing and we came to the base of the northeast ridge of Half Dome itself.

Now it was getting close to 1 p.m. We had been hiking now for seven hours. We only had 400 feet to go, but the final ascent is up the steep rock between two steel cables used as handholds. The cables are fixed with bolts in the rock and raised onto a series of metal poles in what I now call Half Doom! Immediately upon seeing the cables, three in our party turned on their heels and headed back to camp.

My hiking partners for the day were a 16-year-old girl named Holly and an 18-year-old girl named Marylou. Marylou bailed. She took one look at the cables and she was done! She scampered back the way we came. The idea of climbing those cables was scary, so Holly and I decided we would call it quits and head back to camp with Marylou. We decided that at the very least, we would touch the side of Half Dome before leaving. We walked up to the massive granite rock and touched it together. Holly touched it, but then she grabbed the cables and started climbing up. I said, "What are you doing?"

"We got this far… might as well see it all," she said.

I, not to be outdone by a 16-year-old girl, started climbing. I was terrified, and my fear of heights was not helping the situation. I was truly doing the most stupid thing I had ever done. After about 200 feet,

I froze. I looked to each side of that hunk of granite and realized that nothing was preventing me from plummeting to my death. All I could see was open air and stone. I was entertaining the thought of just turning around and getting the heck off that rock.

"Run, you fool!" I was thinking. At about that time, a young man about thirteen years old was coming down and saw me frozen there.

"You have come too far to wimp out now," he said. I grabbed the cables and started the ascent up the hulking cliff – not because of what the boy had said, but because the people behind me were laughing. Up I went with a newfound fury, and I reached the top.

The reward for this uphill, frightening, stressful, painful journey was sheer beauty; a panoramic view of a world that few have seen. There were, 8,000 feet above the valley floor, blue skies, open forest and nothing but the sound of the gentle wind blowing. It was surreal and out of sheer reverence for the spectacular place we now stood, no one spoke above a whisper. No one can appreciate the value of this experience unless he has had the opportunity to make this journey for himself. It was worth every sore muscle, every blister and every drop of sweat.

I am surprised by the number of people who find me somewhat heroic because I decided not to run, but to stick it out with Anna. I find it equally as surprising the number of people who literally called me stupid for staying. I do not view myself as heroic or stupid. I view myself as someone who had a wife whom he loved, who was sick and who was worth it.

When we got married, I took my vows seriously. The vows simply said, "…For better or worse, for richer or poorer and in sickness and health." We did not enter our marriage with a prenuptial agreement that said, *"in sickness and in health… with the following exceptions:*

going crazy is unacceptable – bipolar, depressed or whatever; getting fat will not be tolerated; going bald is acceptable, toupees are not; being grossly disfigured; losing an appendage, loss of sight or hearing before the age of eighty, or going bankrupt. Any or all of the aforementioned conditions will render the contract of marriage null and void, but other than that, I promise to love and to cherish, from this day forward until death do us part."

I know all the Christian arguments on why a Christian person should not get a divorce. I know that adultery is the only biblical reason a Christian would even entertain the idea of divorce. It also teaches grace as well. It was the belief in grace that saved our marriage.

I could have argued that scriptures gave me every right to end the marriage back in 1997. What scripture didn't say is what troubled me. What if your spouse is emotionally disturbed and commits adultery? I could not end this marriage based on the affair. It was not that clear-cut for me. If I focused on myself, maybe that could have been an option, but I didn't focus on myself. I focused on Anna.

I considered that she was sick. That is in no way an excuse, and neither Anna nor I have ever used that as a good reason to dismiss what happened. Anna never used her illness as an excuse. If anyone did, it was me. However, the illness did play a part in the affair, and it needed to be considered. I decided that the best course of action was to extend grace and forgiveness. Yes, I was devastated, and it was a pain I don't ever want to feel again, but I wanted to stay married to Anna. Remember, I said she was worth it, and I wasn't about to place a "scarlet letter" on her. We worked hard because I wanted to remain married and so did she. It took time to work through, and it was not easy, but we made it.

As it turns out, it really was the best course of action. I would learn later that people with bipolar disorder can be seductive and

MUD, BLOOD & CARDBOARD

promiscuous and often participate in dangerous sexual activity. If my focus had been entirely on me, I could have made a big mistake. I would have divorced not *who* hurt our marriage, but *what* hurt it. I wanted a divorce, but not from Anna. I wanted a divorce from the illness. If I had left her, it would have been the equivalent of cutting off my head because I had a headache. I would have divorced the illness, and in the process, lost Anna – the woman I loved and married.

If nothing else, this part of my history taught me that it is always better to err on the side of grace. Grace is receiving a gift or benefit that we don't deserve. I could have been caught up in entitlement and told Anna all the things I deserved and didn't deserve. Instead, I got caught up in grace. I cannot pretend that it was easy to do. I felt that there were things that I was entitled to – like freedom from fear and shame. I needed to be able to trust her.

The challenge to couples who have had the misfortune of broken trust because of an affair or for those who have been hurt for whatever reason, is to try grace and forgiveness before judgment.

Ask a simple question: "Is he/she really worth it?" Most people will answer, "Yes." Even with the pain and betrayal of an affair, most people want to work things out.

I know countless numbers of people who have survived adultery because grace and forgiveness were given first priority. There is always hope. It is possible to rescue and revive a marriage even if there has been unfaithfulness. There is always hope for a closer, more meaningful, romantically passionate marriage. Trust me, it can happen if both parties are willing to embrace grace and forgiveness and let God intervene.

CHAPTER 17

Carving

It was late August in southern California. The temperature was 102 and the humidity was high. It felt like it was 115 outside. It was the season when everyone dressed in shorts, flip-flops and tank tops to accommodate the hot weather. That is, everyone except Anna. She was wearing shorts, tennis shoes and a long-sleeve sweatshirt. Why would she need long sleeves in 102-degree heat? She needed to cover up the lateral slashes that covered the inside of both forearms from wrist to elbow.

Anna was a cutter. She was a self-abuser. The idea of her sitting alone in a bathroom or closet with a razor blade, knife, or anything else that was sharp, and cutting herself was even more difficult for me to accept than the idea of her wanting to commit suicide. I knew that Anna did this in her teenage years, but I never could have guessed that she would do this as an adult. It started again in the spring of 2000.

This is a difficult subject for most people. It is difficult to understand, so before I continue, I feel that I need to spend some time explaining self-abuse. It took me years to understand and grasp why people would do something like this to themselves. It was so unreasonable to me. I just couldn't wrap my mind around it. After asking tons of questions, reading and web-surfing, I have a clearer understanding of what self-abuse is and why a person does this. I am not an expert and I do not have any credentials in psychology, but I lived with a self-abuser, and I have walked this long road with her. That gives me a little insight on the subject.

Self-injury, also known as self-harm and self-mutilation, is the act of deliberately harming your own body, such as cutting or burning yourself. It's not usually associated with an attempt at suicide. Self-injury is an unhealthy way some people, mostly women, cope with overwhelming feelings and emotions. These emotions can be intense stress, anger and frustration that are turned inward.

There is no simple way to explain self-injury. Any combination of emotions can trigger it. In cutting, a person is dealing with deep psychological pain that they can't usually face. For example, a person may have a difficult time handling, expressing or understanding their emotions. The act of causing physical pain can be a distraction from the emotional pain or at least help to give a sense of control over an otherwise uncontrollable situation. In a way, the breaking of skin and the flow of blood brings some temporary relief to someone who is feeling the torture of inner turmoil that cannot be expressed. Self-abusers are emotionally empty; hurting themselves is a way to feel something. Physical pain gives them an external way to express internal distress and despair. In some cases, a self-abuser will hurt themselves as a way to inflict self-punishment to appease guilt for anything that is perceived as being their fault. Self-injury may accompany a variety of mental illnesses, such as depression, eating disorders and borderline personality disorder.

Self-injury is not a failed suicide attempt. I have met so many people that saw their loved ones with scars, bruises and burns, and they immediately thought that those represented failed attempts at taking their lives. It normally is not the case. Self-injury is not a fad or a way for someone just to act out. Though it can be used to get a spouse's or parent's attention, it is still very serious and needs to be addressed. Over the years, different groups of teenagers like goth and emo kids have used cutting as a way of expressing themselves.

A couple of years back, I was at a mall waiting for my bus home. It was just me and a few goth/emo kids keeping me company. One girl was showing off an ace bandage wrapped around her wrist. This, of course, captured my attention. A teenage boy with his black eyeliner and jet-black hair looked at her wrist and asked, "What's with the bandage?"

She replied very matter-of-factly, "I cut." The group nodded with understanding as she rubbed her wrist for dramatic effect. I, being a caring and nosy person, had to know more.

"So, you cut yourself?" I inquired of the young lady dressed in tight black jeans and a Black Crows t-shirt. She looked at me defiantly and snapped, "Yeah! Why do you care?"

"Well, it really is none of my business, but my wife is a cutter and is in the hospital right now because of it."

"I didn't try to kill myself," she fired back at me, as the whole group now fixed its attention on our conversation.

"I didn't say that she tried to kill herself. I said that she was a cutter like you."

She looked around at all her emo friends for support and stated, "We all cut. We all need to cut, and we have to in order to feel."

I nodded and looked at them all. I was getting ready to make my point. "Can I see your scars then?"

"What kind of sick bastard are you, man? You want to see our scars?"

"Yes, I do. I just want to see the scars of your tortured emotions."

"Fine," said the girl with the bandaged wrist. She unwrapped the bandage, which revealed two scratches that were about three inches long. A kitten could have delivered a more deadly cut. I let out a long whistle to show my amazement. "Impressive… Who else has a scar?" I asked the rest of the group. A couple of the other kids showed me a couple of marks that were one to two inches long that were barely visible.

"Wow guys, you would love my wife. She has slashes from wrist to bicep on both arms. Some of them are not even fully healed yet."

"*That is sick, man!* Your wife does that to herself? That is crazy!" One of the other girls said, and she looked even paler than she looked a few seconds before.

"Yes, she is very ill, but she is getting help for what is going on up here," I said, pointing to my head. For the next few minutes, we discussed the real deal of self-abuse, and I explained that doing what they were pretending to do was very serious, and that unless they truly had severe issues, they shouldn't do it. We discussed their "horrible" lives and how they hated living. I encouraged them to choose healthy ways to express themselves though music, poetry or writing. They all agreed, and I watched as they were picked up by their horrible parents and continued on with their horrible lives. They left via Lexus, Land Rovers and Navigators. As I watched the last car drive away, I looked down. The girl with the bandage on her wrist had left her bandage behind. Seems it wasn't important to her anymore.

According to Anna and a few other people I have had the honor of talking to about this, all self-injury does is bring a very temporary calmness and a release of tension. This will always result in guilt and shame. A person who is already dealing with a painful emotional state now has this guilt on top of what they were already trying to deal with. Because self-injury is impulsive, it is very difficult to control. Anna felt that it was addictive as well, because it does bring that temporary relief.

Anna called it "carving." I hated that term. It just made it worse. She would tell me, "I want to carve." Putting it like that made it even more "icky" than I thought it was.

Remember, I didn't have a good grasp on this anyway, and her casual way of telling me that she wanted to "carve" on herself made me feel sick and angry. I would tell her, "Well, don't do that. That is stupid." Way to be supportive, huh? I hated this more than anything else, and Anna knew it. I did a lot wrong when it came to this issue. I belittled, yelled, swore and criticized her for doing it. I took on the role of a mean parent rather than a supportive husband.

She would try and hide it from me. I'd find out. The sweatshirts in August sort of gave it away. It was a little embarrassing being at family functions when she would wear long sleeves or sweatshirts. We lived in southern California; there was no need for long sleeves. But she was covering up a habit and a behavior that she could not help or control. Eventually, I got it. I understood why she did it. At least I didn't stay an idiot. I educated myself and became the supportive spouse I needed to be.

Why did Anna do this? Well, why was Anna the way she was at all? Why does a person "go crazy" or have a "nervous breakdown?" It has to do with the person's whole life, not just the present situation. You have to go all the way back to May 9, 1970, and retrace Anna's life journey to the present to understand. In order to know and understand Anna, you have to go back thirty years and meet Annie.

CHAPTER 18

Annie

Everyone called her Annie. Her mother was a legal secretary working for a successful lawyer. Their affair would produce a child, and in May 1970, Annie had arrived to take her place in this world.

Her parents ended two prior marriages and destroyed both families in order to begin their new life and family with Annie. She was very fortunate to be granted an instant older brother and three older sisters from her mother's side of the marriage. She was not so fortunate with her father's family. The divorce had produced very strained relationships between his ex-wife and Anna's half-sister, whom she had never met. Even with the rough history with their previous families, Anna's parents provided a stable, loving family. Annie's beginnings were more than ideal.

She was the star of the show whenever her brother and sisters were around. Daddy was the definition of love and affection to Annie. Mommy was playful and loving as any Mom would be. A year and two months later, Annie's little brother, Aaron, was born.

Daddy was Annie and little Aaron's hero. He would play his cello for them and teach them "My Bonnie Lies over the Ocean" and "Home on the Range." Every time he returned home from a trip, he would have presents of some sort, and he loved to shower them with kisses. Mommy would bake them cookies, tickle their feet and love them as any Mom should. It was paradise. Family vacations were so exciting for Annie and little Aaron. They would be awakened when the sun was still down and be carried to a large Winnebago, and after being carefully laid in their camper beds, Daddy and Mommy would sip coffee and drive. When the sun came up, they would stop for pancakes and chocolate milk. Their family was so loving and so exciting. Annie and little Aaron loved their lives together.

For six years, Annie lived a great life of excitement, vacations and love. For six years, Annie would know no want, no hurt and no sorrow. Then, at age six, Annie and little Aaron were called into the front room of their home. Mommy was there and she sat them on a couch across from her.

"Your father has died," she announced.

That was it. Just four words to her children of six and five years of age. "Your father has died." She did not comfort them or pull them into her lap. She just stared at them and said the four most awful words Annie had ever heard in six short years. After the news, she sent Annie and Aaron outside to play. They went to a friend's house a block away and told them the news. Little Aaron climbed into his friend's Mommy's lap and cried uncontrollably for several hours. Annie said nothing and would not be consoled; she just stared out the window with her thoughts.

This was the end of Annie's happy life. No more exciting vacations, no more cello, no more songs, and worst of all, no more Daddy. Annie and little Aaron had to get up and put on fancy clothes for the funeral. Annie was forced to wear a dress and little Aaron a tie. Annie did not feel like dressing up for this day. It was a bad day and no one understood how miserable she was since her daddy died. It seemed to Annie that Mommy was not that upset about Daddy's death; she almost seemed happy about it.

Her only display of emotion was at the funeral when she hung out of the limo and wailed so everyone could see her display of grief. Annie doesn't remember very much about Daddy's funeral service. Green grass and people standing around a big tree and the soldiers folding the American flag is all she remembers. After the funeral, the grownups all went to Annie's house to have food and cocktails. Annie was very sad, and she hated that everyone was laughing and telling stories.

"This is no time for laughing. My daddy has died! How can they laugh?" Annie thought to herself. The funeral was just the beginning. It was not the worst part of Daddy's death. After the funeral, Annie and little Aaron hoped that somehow Daddy would come home. They wished that one day he'd come through the front door and kiss them and bring them gifts. Annie would sit and stare into nothingness while little Aaron cried and carried Daddy's shirt around with him. Mommy made no time to address Annie's pain and grief, nor little Aaron's. It was back to business as usual. The two children would be left on their own to deal with their horrible pain.

Mommy changed. She was not the Mommy they knew while Daddy was alive. She became distant and less interested in her two children. With daddy gone, she seemed to drop the Mommy routine over time, and she became Mother. As time pushed forward, Mother grew more distant and less affectionate. By the time Annie was in elementary school, Mother worked until dark, then came home and locked herself in her room where she smoked long cigarettes and drank instant coffee. Mother never went to open house at school, a school play or a parent-teacher conference. She was Mother by name only.

Mother's distant and emotionless behavior was not the worst of it. Soon she became mean-spirited and overbearing. She demanded that Annie and little Aaron show no emotion. Regular childlike behavior was not acceptable. Noise, laughter, crying, or playing over-exuberantly was not tolerated. They were expected to act like adults. Sit still, hands in laps and no fidgeting.

Mother didn't just drift away emotionally; she became abusive, both emotionally and physically. Annie and little Aaron were severely punished for breaking the rules.

The problem with the rules was that the rules were never clearly defined and often changed with Mother's mood. This meant that anything and everything could constitute a breach in protocol, and that always meant punishment. Annie and little Aaron never knew when and if they would be breaking a rule, so they decided to treat everything as if they could be in trouble.

They lived in fear. In those days, Mother worked late and usually did not get home until after dark. Annie and Aaron were not allowed to touch any food until she came home. There were times where there was no food in the house at all. Annie and Aaron did creative things like chew peanuts up and spit them out on bread to create their own peanut butter. Disgusting, yes, but they did what they needed to do to quench the hunger. They didn't dare touch anything in the kitchen or Mother would punish them.

One day, Annie's sister came to visit. It was always good to see her older brother and sisters. She brought Annie a doll that she loved. Not long after the visit, Annie was playing with her new doll. Her mother came into the room and asked, "Where did you get that doll?"

"Debbie gave it to me," Annie replied.

"Are you sure?" Mother shot back with a look of disdain.

Annie burst out in tears. She knew that she would be punished because Mother always forgot things, and that usually meant a spanking.

"Yes! I am sure," Annie exclaimed through the tears.

"Okay, Debbie gave it to you."

With a toss of her head and a grin, Mother walked away, leaving Annie standing there clutching her doll, sobbing. It was the game that seemed to be the most important thing to Mother. She was a controlling woman who, surprisingly, never raised her voice, but she could scream in a whisper and strike fear into the hearts of her children in a very calm, yet sadistic way.

Annie was hit by a car at age eleven. It knocked her down, and she hit her head pretty hard. There would be severe punishment if Mother found out. Annie kept her accident secret out of the fear of what Mother would do to her. Mother never took Annie to the doctor. Not for a check-up, or even when the school nurse sent word home that Annie had scoliosis. Annie and little Aaron would not visit their first dentist until they moved away from Mother. When Annie had an asthma attack so bad that she thought she would die, all Mother did was stand in the doorway and watch her wheeze uncontrollably. There were some home remedies, but no real medical attention.

Mother was prone to spontaneous cleaning frenzies that were grueling and always involved Annie and Aaron. There was no warning, just orders to clean the garage, or to do yard work or to clean some other room. Mother's project always took hours to accomplish and usually ended up in punishment from Mother because Anna and Aaron did something either incorrectly or too slowly. During one of Mother's cleaning frenzies, she had Annie and Aaron up early to clean up the yard. The task for the day for an 11-year-old and a 12-year-old was to remove two Bird of Paradise plants.

Mother did not give them any direction. They were forced to use whatever rusty tool they could find in the garage. An axe was the tool of choice for Annie. After taking several swings at the plant, Annie sunk the axe deeply into her leg. Blood went everywhere and pain shot through her body. Quickly, Annie and Aaron ran to the back of the house and snuck in the back door to their rooms. They quickly taped up the leg and covered up the injury with a new pair of jeans. The scar it left on Annie's leg is huge. This should have received medical attention, but Mother had created so much fear in her children that they would not tell her about the injury.

When Mother punished, it was more to inflict pain than it was to correct. Mother's beatings were done with a belt, a coat hanger, electrical cord or with a shoe. It was never done in moderation, but always in excess. Anna described it to me as "a beating until my Mother's arm was tired, and then she switched hands and hit me until that arm was tired."

Birthdays and Christmas meant nothing to Mother. She simply treated them like any other day. No special attention, no parties and no cake. Barely a "happy birthday" came from Mother.

On Mother's birthday, when Annie was just eleven years old, Annie wanted to make Mother a birthday card out of construction paper and ribbon. Mother was resting on the sofa and Annie asked for permission to use the materials for the card. Annie was very proud of her card and brought it to Mother with a smile. Mother snatched the card away from Annie.

"Where did you get the supplies to make this?" she asked.

"I asked you if I could use them," Annie replied, a little confused.

At this, Mother threw the birthday card away and proceeded to severely beat Annie from head to ankles for not making sure that Mother was awake enough when asking for permission to use her supplies.

Annie lived her entire childhood and into her adult life in fear of Mother and in emotional pain. Annie was withdrawn, sad and lonely. She suppressed every emotion and rarely cried. At age sixteen, Annie and Aaron went to live with their sister and finally broke free from Mother. She didn't get away soon enough.

One afternoon, at age twelve, Annie found herself alone in the garage when her older brother's friend walked in. A 12-year-old girl should not have to be the victim of an 18-year-old's perversions, but she was. This proved to be the last externally painful event in Anna's life, and she soon turned her pain inward and began what she called carving. This behavior lasted a few years, and she didn't do it again until she was thirty years old.

Annie grew up and became Anna somewhere in the process. Anna was a wife and a mother whose adult life started much like her childhood – happy, loving and ideal. She faced something very painful that she could not control when her father passed away at age six. As an adult, she faced more pain that she could not control, born out of everything that she had experienced from age six to present day. Out of control and losing herself, Anna practically lived in a mental hospital for several years. Annie grew up to be Anna, an adult with mental illness: Anna the mental patient.

CHAPTER 19

The Fear of the Unknown

I think the worst part of being married to a person with a mental disability is the uncertainty in your life. Having a mentally unstable family member means that you have an unstable home. Every family has some form of dysfunction, but for a family dealing with a mental illness, it means that dysfunction is in your face every day. There is no break, no lapse in the difficulty and no easy part. It is hard work and every day brings the unknown.

I would get up every day and not know what was going to happen. If Anna was at home, I did not know if Anna would be happy or sad. I did not know if she would want to get out and do something or if she would just want to stay in bed. Some days she would be ready to take on the world, clean, cook and pay bills, and had the energy to do anything and everything. Most days she just sat and did nothing.

Holidays, birthdays, the start of school, summer vacations, winter break or spring vacation were all triggers that meant that Anna had about a ninety percent chance of a return visit to the hospital. It got to where I would just plan on it. The anniversary of her father's death also proved to be a trigger.

Family functions scared Anna to death. She hated holidays anyway, so the idea of going to a family gathering was hell for her. On some holidays, she would be excited that we were all going to be together and faced them with great anticipation. I never knew what was going to happen. There were many Thanksgivings and Christmases when Anna would beg me to just let her stay home. I was always afraid of what might happen if I did let her stay home. I feared coming home from a family celebration to find that she had finally succeeded at taking her own life. I was afraid that my children would have to have a holiday as a marker of their mother's death for the rest of their lives. I know that is an awful way to think, but that is how it was back then.

If Anna was in the hospital, I would get up every day still not knowing what the day would bring. I would have to wait to get the 8 a.m. phone call from her to get a feel for what I was in for. Some days it was pleasant and we would discuss what I could bring for her when I visited later that evening. Some days she was depressed and didn't want to talk to me or see me. I used to wait for the phone call, and if I didn't get one, it meant something was up. Those days were torture for me. I would have to call and track her down. Sometimes it just meant that she forgot. Sometimes this meant that she was feeling better and was caught up in a television show or a conversation.

Most of the time, however, this meant trouble, and I would find out that she had acted out or done something that had landed her back in ICU. I hated the wait for that phone call. I was in constant fear that she would kill herself. In those days, I got up at 4 a.m., so that meant I had to wait for four hours before I knew if my wife was alive or not. I hated that wait for a good reason. It is sort of a compound feeling of fear, death, hopelessness and panic all rolled up into one.

In the meantime, I was growing more unstable myself. I had started smoking cigarettes and cigars, and I had begun to drink a lot. I found that any alcoholic beverage was an effective pain medication for my woes. This was strange because I went from being a non-drinking pastor to a booze-it-up-daily shipyard worker. I was dealing with my mentally ill wife and dealing with my own mental turmoil.

I was so obsessed with what had happened to me with Pastor Rich, I spent hours sitting and fantasizing about how I could kill him. I was so filled with hatred that I wanted him dead. It was never a quick death, either. I wanted to beat and maim and hurt him. I felt so screwed over and somehow I blamed him for everything. I blamed him for my misery and Anna's condition. He had forced me to be this way. In my mind, it was completely his fault.

In reality, it was not all his fault. His betrayal was terrible, but he didn't cause Anna's illness. He was not torturing me and making me miserable. I was so angry and obsessed with him that it was making me sick emotionally.

I was lost. Smoking and drinking were now my gods and my life was far from the real God. Rudy was dead and buried deep within himself. The new Rudy was on the loose and was miserable, self-loathing and possibly homicidal.

CHAPTER 20

One Hit Man and a Side of Manly Man

"You've got to be freaking kidding me! You want to do what?"

Stu, my good friend of many years, was chiding me over a glass of Merlot in his living room.

"I didn't say that I wanted to do it," I said. "I said I think about it a lot. If I could, I might."

"You are serious!"

"I guess."

"You're a freaking idiot!"

Stu was the type of guy that did not mince words. A former male escort, pimp, drug dealer, bouncer, and I think he may have been a sort of hit man, Stu had a résumé of illegal activity that would make your head swim. I met him in the eighties in the shipyards. In the days that followed, he and his wife gave their hearts to Christ… but Stu wasn't a normal run-of-the-mill Christian. When Stu became a follower of Christ he was a new guy, but he still swore profusely and was generally a no-nonsense man. We became good friends because of our love for pro wrestling and because we admired each others' style and wit. We also had a lack of patience for "stupid people," and would rather punch them than listen to their crap. He called us the B.S.F.C.: Body Slammers for Christ. He was more of a "body slammer" than I was. I witnessed him hit a guy so hard for making fun of his faith that I thought the guy was dead. Not the best way to present Christ, but sometimes I think we Christians need more people like him around.

It was to this 6'6" fellow "Body Slammer" that I confessed that I wanted to commit murder. He sat there in his living room, his blue eyes fixed on me, burning with indignation. I felt his irritation with our conversation, and I could only hope that the next part of the discussion wouldn't result in him hauling off and knocking me out.

"What is wrong with you, dude?" he said. "You are not just thinking or fantasizing about killing this idiot. You have allowed this thing to put murder in your heart."

Now I wanted to hit Stu. I expected a little solidarity here. Here was a guy who had the same hard, caustic, mean-spirited heart that I did. I wanted some validation, not realistic reason. Then he told me a personal story that resulted in him ending a man's life many years ago. It was the result of a situation similar to mine, but he actually did what I was fantasizing about. After finishing his story, he looked at me.

"Look, I've whacked a lot of guys and most of them deserved it, but I am not so sure that guy did," he said with the same matter-of-fact manner a person might use to talk about a first kiss.

"So you think I have murder in my heart? That is an interesting perspective," I said.

"Uh…yeah, 'Reverend'… It is interesting to me that you would throw away everything you have to even consider this. He isn't even worth a second thought. He's in your head, man, and you need to get him out."

I sat there staring at the wall, digesting what Stu was saying. I was certainly taking a path in the wrong direction, and I needed to let it go.

Stu was right, and he was the first person to bring some clarity to me. I decided right there in his living room that I was not going to entertain any more fantasies of violent acts. The only problem was I couldn't stop them by myself. I needed help.

I drove to my first therapy appointment with a knot in my stomach. I didn't like the idea of going to see a mental health professional because I didn't think that I needed to be there. I knew that what I was about to go and talk about could land me in the Funny Farm with my wife, and there are just some things that married couples don't have to do together – like hunting, golfing, quilting, and being admitted to a mental hospital.

My new therapist called my name and escorted me into his office. It was a nice office, warmly decorated with candles and perfect colors to make me feel relaxed and at ease. I felt like taking a nap the minute I walked in.

We went over some preliminary paperwork and started our forty-five minute session. He was a great guy. He was soft-spoken, but he held onto his masculinity. I liked this because some of the male therapists I had met in the past were so sweet and spoke with such kind words that it made me a bit uncomfortable. We made small talk and then he asked, "So why are you here today?"

It was my turn to take control of the conversation, so I did. I looked him square in the eyes and stated, "Look, I know how this works. If I tell you I am going to hurt myself, I am getting a free trip to the Funny Farm. If I tell you that I am going to hurt someone else, same deal applies. I have an issue, and I need to know that you are not going to freak out and sound some alarm and have me carted away."

He looked at me with a slight smile. I think maybe he was trying not to laugh, but he said, "Do you want to hurt yourself?"

"No! Not in any way, shape or form. I have an issue with someone else."

"So you want to hurt someone?" he asked, scribbling something on his legal pad.

"Probably… yeah… I'm not sure."

"Is it anyone close to you, like in your family?"

"No, of course not!"

"Does this person live close to you?"

"No," I said, shaking my head. "He lives a couple hundred miles away."

"Do you have a plan?" he said as he set his pen down and looked at me.

"Yeah, I have a one-step plan… it consists of me coming to see you. I have been entertaining fantasies about brutally hurting or even killing this guy. He did some things a couple of years ago and I am consumed by them."

Dr. "Manly-Man" looked at me from his chair, gave me a smile and said, "That's a good plan. I guess I can cancel the SWAT-team and the straight jacket." We laughed for a few seconds, and I felt relieved. I was glad I had kept my appointment. I knew I was in good hands.

"So Rudy, can you tell me who it is?"

"Yes, I can tell you. The only way to describe him is… well, he is my former pastor, a former mentor and my former friend." I let it all out. The entire Rudy-and-Anna epic tale came flowing out of me like a cattle auctioneer. I don't think I took a breath for thirty minutes. It felt good to talk about it, and it was also good to have some neutral person to hear from. We scheduled an appointment for the following week and I went home with at least a little hope. I counseled with Dr. Manly-Man for about six weeks, and I learned about anger management, healthy mental pictures, distorted thoughts and tons of good stuff. At the end of six weeks, my murderous, unrealistic thoughts were now merely thoughts of yelling and screaming at Pastor Rich. The hatred and bitterness were still there, and I was still consumed by the whole ordeal, but now I was at least more realistic about it.

Stu the hit-man and Dr. Manly-Man were two people that God used to save me from myself. If Stu had not pointed me toward the futility in my thinking, I never would have found the wisdom in those therapy sessions. I was still too far gone at the time to realize that God was there protecting me from myself, providing what I needed. He was there to protect me from my own stupidity.

CHAPTER 21

Shock Option

Sometimes life can deliver something that no one could have imagined you would have to face. Shock treatment was somewhere on the bottom of the list of likely things I'd face or have to make a decision about. Life didn't care about my list and neither did Anna's doctors. Anna's doctor suggested shock treatment because she was not responding to any of the many medications she had been prescribed. I think at one point Anna was taking up to eight different meds a day. When this seemed to be failing, the "shock option" was presented.

When Anna first presented the idea to me, I was appalled. All I could think of was the shock treatment scene from *One Flew over the Cuckoo's Nest*. The scene shows the character R.P. Murphy innocently lying on a table, surrounded by hospital staff, when he is given a small zap of electricity which electrocutes his brain, causing a violent convulsion. It is sort of a white-knuckle moment every time I watch the movie. The scene leaped into my mind when Anna's doctor suggested that she be given this treatment. A whole lot of people have asked me, "Why did you let her have E.C.T?" I finally started responding to this question with, "Because electrocution of the brain was something that made perfect sense to us." That usually shuts people up. I no longer tell people this part of the story if I don't need to.

The truth is that we were both desperate and I was scared. I didn't want anything to do with E.C.T. I thought for sure that we would be searing in the crazy, much like you sear a steak to seal in the flavor! Nevertheless, over a period of about three months, we made the decision to do the E.C.T.

It was a very difficult and emotional decision. Anna was willing to do anything to feel better and I was willing to give anything a try to get our life back to normal. I have to give her doctor and the hospital staff props for being very helpful and informative. They let us make the decision without pressure. We were shown a video that was sort of a before and after example of people who had experienced E.C.T. By the end of the video, I was sold. I saw some of the most severely ill people return to normal, productive people and that is what I wanted so much for Anna. Anna wanted to return to who and what she was – a Mom, a wife and a happy person. She was tired of dealing with the dark cloud of depression looming overhead. After the video and more counseling, she was scheduled for E.C.T. the following week.

For the first time in what seemed like an eternity, Anna and I had hope. We had hope because for the first time since it all started, some-one actually had a possible solution. It was very possible that after a few treatments, Anna would return home and things could be like they once were. It was 2001. We had been riding this rollercoaster with no breaks for five years. We were ready for the ride to be over. I was seeing the beginning of the end. It felt good.

Electroconvulsive therapy (E.C.T.) is a procedure in which a patient is shocked in the temple area of the head and electrical currents pass through the brain, deliberately triggering a short seizure. Mental health professionals believe this can cause the brain's chemistry to change and alleviate symptoms of certain mental illnesses.

The procedure is quite different today than when it was introduced seventy years ago. Years ago, the treatment was brutal and inhumane, using high doses of electricity and no anesthesia. This type of treatment led to severe memory loss and even death. Today, electroconvulsive therapy does have side effects, but it now uses precisely calculated electrical currents that are administered in a safe and controlled setting. A muscle relaxant and anesthesia are given to the patient prior to treatment.

The E.C.T. treatment is most commonly recommended for people with severe depression, accompanied by psychosis, suicidal tendencies, and unimproved mania and schizophrenia when symptoms are severe or medications are ineffective. Because E.C.T. can provide significant improvement of symptoms faster than psychotherapy or medications, it very well could be the best treatment option in some cases. We took a chance and hoped that E.C.T. could be the answer. However, the side effects are severe and life-changing. It took us three months to make the decision because of the nature of the possible side effects. The first side effect that we were concerned with was *cognitive impairment*. Immediately after an E.C.T. treatment, there is a period of confusion. You do not know where you are or why you're there. This generally lasts from a few minutes to several hours.

For the very first treatment, I took off work and made sure that I was there when Anna woke up from the anesthesia. She woke up and looked around, obviously confused. I took her hand and whispered, "You're fine, you are in the hospital, and you had E.C.T. You are fine." She looked up to me and said, "Yeah... but who are you?" This scared me to death. I thought for sure they had fried her brain. Within seconds, she remembered me, but couldn't remember what had happened earlier that morning.

The doctors assured us that long-term memory loss does not happen and that all memory loss was temporary. Well, that was not true. Anna did not remember anything from before treatment on the days of treatment. She had to write herself notes to remind her of anything that might have been important. She found later that she didn't remember anything throughout the week either, so she kept a notepad to write reminders for herself.

Anna had a total of fifteen treatments, three times a week for five weeks. We were assured that memory problems would improve within a couple of months and that permanent memory loss was rare. Not so with Anna. Her memory loss is quite significant and now, nearly nine years later, she still can't remember conversations I have had with her only a few days before. She has difficulty remembering faces, which can be embarrassing. We went to a friend's church recently, and on our name-tags we were supposed to write our favorite song from high school. Anna could not remember her favorite or a single song from that era. I felt her embarrassment and tried to help her think of a song. It's painful to watch your wife feel embarrassed about something that she can't help.

Come to find out, the most common side effects of E.C.T. are memory loss and cognitive damage. The psychology profession has denied such effects for decades. However, they are finally beginning to acknowledge that memory loss and cognitive damage do occur more frequently than originally believed.

I am not really a proponent of E.C.T. This is mostly due to the adverse effects that it had on Anna. Looking back, do we believe that we did the right thing? Yes. We took a chance that the good things would outweigh the side effects and that everything would be all right. By the way, it was not all right. The E.C.T. did not work, not even a little.

CHAPTER 22

Hope and a Lack Thereof

"To love means loving the unlovable.
To forgive means pardoning the unpardonable.
Faith means believing the unbelievable.
Hope means hoping when everything seems hopeless."

--G.K. Chesterton

The E.C.T. didn't work, and if anything, it may have made things worse. After the treatments, Anna became agitated, impatient and irritable. When the procedure that was supposed to fix her failed, hope failed. Her trips to the hospital increased, her suicidal feelings increased, and the carving/cutting increased and she started on a path of antics that nearly drove me to the funny farm.

Part of the problem was that Anna did some of the things she did because of her mild regression to a junior-higher. Now, I don't know if this is an official diagnosis or not, but we will both agree that she did regress to a rebellious 13-year-old with an extremely selfish attitude. If things did not go her way, she would act out and say and do things that were incredibly harmful to herself and to the relationships she had with people around her.

Anna's first act of rebellion actually took place the very first time that she was hospitalized back in 1997. She and a couple other patients hopped a fence and went swimming in the hospital pool one evening.

This may have been harmless, but for Anna, the quiet introvert, it was strange behavior. This particular time it was no harm no foul because, believe it or not, they did not get caught. What I found strange was that Anna was so very proud of herself for doing this. She thought it was fun and exciting. I thought that it was a silly thing for adults to do. I always have wondered how three suicidal mental patients were able to sneak into a hospital pool unnoticed in the middle of the night. It was really just three people doing something that made them feel alive again, having one moment in their lives when they could feel free, have a laugh and do something exciting. Even though I sort of scolded Anna for doing it, I am glad she did.

As the illness progressed, she did things to take back her childhood. She would see those very large piles of dirt on construction sites and then return after hours with a friend and a cardboard box to slide down them. Why? Because they are there… and she didn't get to do that when she was a kid.

These things were not acts during a manic episode or some psychotic breakdown; they were simply a woman doing something to blow off a little steam. Unconventional, yes, but I was still glad she did it. If a moment of fun can bring some joy to a mostly painful life, then who cares if she is off playing in the dirt? I didn't.

During Anna's trips to the hospital during the 2000 to 2004 period, her regressions were much worse and disturbing. Her rebellion would first take place by "cheeking" her medication. This is a trick that patients use to store up their medication. They pretend to take their medication by hiding their pills in their cheek and collect a stockpile of pills to take in the future to overdose with. The sad reality was that Anna had convinced herself that she was a nuisance to me and her children and that we were better off without her. This was a cry for help, but it was really an indicator of how desperate she was. To make matters much worse, every time she would act out in the hospital, she would get tossed back into ICU. This always enraged her. If there was one place on the planet that she hated, it was the ICU, but like a rebellious teenager, she would do one thing after another that would get her thrown back where she didn't want to be.

If my memory serves me correctly, Anna did this a few times. On one of those times, she decided to hang herself by using her bed sheets and throwing them over a pipe in the ceiling. I was grateful that she didn't succeed, but I was angry that she had made the attempt. I usually found out by calling her and finding out that she was back in ICU. When I would see her or talk to her on the phone, I would be having a conversation with Anna the 13-year-old. She would blame everyone else for what she had done. She would not look at me and would answer every question with, "I don't know."

Patients were also rewarded for good behavior. When patients improved and did well, they could get a pass from their doctor that allowed them to have meals off the floor in the hospital cafeteria. Here, patients could have dinner with their families. This was a nice privilege for the family as well as for the patient. I loved it. Yes, it was hospital cafeteria food, but it was a time that I could eat and visit with my wife. I would bring the kids there from time to time so we could eat dinner or lunch together as a family. It was nice.

There were even times when I was allowed to escort Anna off the wing myself and we would walk the grounds and visit or eat together. On the weekends, I would bring the kids and our dog to visit. It just gave our family an hour to be normal and sit outside on a bench and laugh and play with the dog. We all loved it. That is why I would get so angry when Anna would do something that revoked all her privileges.

There was the time that Anna went to lunch in the cafeteria and stole a couple of pins from a bulletin board and scratched up her arms in a cutting episode. She then went back in ICU and lost all her privileges. No more cafeteria visits.

Now, these acts always resulted in a trip to ICU and often resulted in phone calls from Anna demanding that I come and take her home. This was in no way an option because once a doctor has placed a patient in a mental health facility, it comes with a legal hold for anywhere from forty-eight hours to weeks. I could not come to get her and take her home if I wanted to. But I would still get the raging phone call telling me that she had to get out of there and I was to come and get her at once. I would try to reason with her, but if I did not agree with her, I would get screamed at, hung up on, or cussed out. I was even accused of being part of a plot to keep her locked away forever. Then there were the attempts at guilt.

"You don't care about me!"

"You don't love me!"

"You don't ever want me to come home!"

"You hate me!"

These attempts at guilt worked for about thirty seconds, and I would just let her rail at me. When dealing with a person with a mental illness, you learn to pick and choose whom you get angry with. I should say "what" you get angry with. It was never Anna that was railing at me with great disdain, it was the illness. Whenever the unreasonable, selfish acts appeared, the best thing to do was ignore it. Just letting her go through what she was going through and not reacting to her diffused the situation. She would get so angry at me that she would slam the phone down and refuse to call me for hours and sometimes days. More often than not, I would just give her a few hours and call back. Afterward, she would take the call and we would move on.

Anna did not limit her antics to the hospital. She pulled some real zingers at home, as well. My favorite of these events was the evening that I came home around 10 p.m. and Anna was in bed, reading. It seemed that all was well. I went into the bathroom to get ready for bed. In the distance, I could hear the sirens of police cars, fire trucks and ambulances. I thought to myself, "They seem to be getting close to us."

There was a huge hill that led up to our apartment complex from the main street, and I could definitely hear them coming up our hill. They were coming up the hill to our complex with all the bells and whistles blaring. I was an assistant manager of the complex, so my next step was to go outside to see where on earth they were going. I threw on a shirt to run outside to see who was in trouble. The loud knock on my front door stopped me cold. They were at my door!

I answered it and there stood two paramedics, three firemen and a police officer. Behind them, I could see the red lights flashing. The scene was almost surreal because I didn't know why they were at my door. The look on my face must have been priceless because the looks on their faces were.

Policeman: "We got a call that there was a suicide attempt?"

Me: "No, I didn't call."

Fireman: "This is apartment 25, right?"

Me: "Yeah, but I didn't call you."

Paramedic: "We got a 911-call from a suicide hotline."

All of them were looking at me like a murder suspect, and I was so confused that I just stood there looking at them with what had to be the stupidest look on my face. Then, from the bedroom came a small, timid voice.

"That's probably my fault." She had called a hotline because she was not feeling very well and had hoped that they would make her feel better. The person that Anna spoke with was a little too aggressive for her, and she hung up on the social worker on the other end. This, of course, raised questions, and the authorities were dispatched. Once Anna explained the situation and convinced everyone that she was fine, they left. I was absolutely mortified. The questions from the neighbors lasted for days.

My least favorite was the night that Anna went for a walk. This was not an uncommon event. She would often take a walk to burn off energy and just get away for a little while. On this particular night, she left right after dinner and an hour later, she had not returned. After an hour and a half, she still was not home, and I went to look for her. I did not find her. I walked to the end of the drive and looked down the hill to see if she was coming home. I did this for two or three hours. I called the police and made a missing person's report. They were helpful, but not hopeful.

I was awake most of the evening and finally fell asleep around 2 a.m. I was up and 6 a.m. and no Anna. I was scared to death. The kids were too, even though I tried my best to keep things on an upbeat, positive note. At 8:30 a.m., she called. She was in the hospital again. She decided to call an ambulance because she felt suicidal, and they came and took her back. I was not happy. I was so angry at her for doing that. To this day, I don't know why she did that. It is not something that either one of us understands.

I would like to tell you that I reacted to her difficult behavior with the proper response every time. I would like to tell you that, but the truth is I did not. I often reacted very negatively to her episodes, especially when she carved herself up or made an attempt at taking her own life. You have to remember that I was not in a good place at this time and was dealing with my own personal issues. I was still feeling very betrayed, and I was bitter. When Anna did something that I didn't like, I would sometimes respond by accusing her of not trying or of being a quitter. I would become so outraged over her self-loathing acts that I would refuse to talk to her. The very idea of her doing things that kept her away from me and the children infuriated me. It also scared me so badly that I didn't know of any other way to react but to get upset and make unrealistic accusations. Anna will tell you that there were times when I acted crazier than she ever did, and she is right.

Fear is a strange and unpredictable emotion. It can cause us to do and say things that make us look like we are insane if we let it take over and control our lives. That is what it did to me. Well, in my own defense, do you blame me for being scared? My wife wanted to take her own life, and she was continually carving up and cutting her arms. I didn't even know who she was anymore. Every time the phone rang and the caller I.D. showed the hospital's name, I knew that it could either be Anna wanting to talk, or it could be the hospital informing me that she was dead.

I feared for myself and I feared for my kids. The problem is I let all the fear, the betrayal, the anger and bitterness get the best of me. I let it become the ruler of my life. At the very least, I should have been in control of myself and not my very unstable emotions. At the very best, I should have had faith in God. But to me, He had disappeared a long time ago, so fear, anger and bitterness were my guides. Self-protection was the key. No one could be allowed to hurt me, scare me, or make me feel insecure. I had to protect myself, and I had to protect my kids, too. I had made some resolve here, and in some ways that was good, but it was the author of this resolve that nullified it. Fear was my prime motivator and this only caused more problems. My thoughts were unclear and distorted. None of my thinking was based in reality. I was paranoid. I had turned inward and no one on the outside of me was allowed in except my children. My ability to see things objectively no longer existed. Hope was gone. Hope had failed.

CHAPTER 23

Drowning

I didn't know that I was in over my head. I didn't realize how far I had drifted into the deep ocean of despair. I had been trying to emotionally tread water for so long that I was weak and no longer had the strength to fight the currents. I was sinking. I was drowning in bitterness, drowning in despair, drowning in hopelessness. I was having physical episodes where I felt that I couldn't breathe. My head would spin and I would lie in my bed at night and feel like I was dying, gasping. Yep, I was having panic attacks. I was not just deteriorating; I was damaged, broken and certainly undone.

My condition and state of mind made me feel vulnerable. I did not tell a soul what was happening to me. Some people who are close to me are probably learning about this part of the story for the first time as they read this. I covered it all up very well. I was in this sad state for a very long time.

It was during this time that Anna came home from the hospital. I was always relieved when she came home. It made my world feel better when she was home. The problem was, the woman who came home looked like Anna, but she was not Anna at all. For close to a week, a strange, moody, argumentative, dark woman was living in my home. The stress was unbearable. I did not know what was going on with her.

On a Friday night, it all just came to a miserable breaking point. Like I said, she was not a very pleasant person to be around, and after a disagreement, she stormed off to sulk in the bedroom. I was so tired of her complaining and voicing how she hated our home and hated having to do anything. I just wanted her to help with the kids or just do a load of laundry. This particular time, I asked her to cook dinner and she stormed off. Her comment under her breath was, "I hate this place." This pushed my button and I followed her to the bedroom and said, "If you are so miserable here with me and the kids, then get the <bleep> out!"

So she did. She put her shoes on and walked out.

It was hard to know exactly what was going on in Anna's head at that moment, but I have to admit that I was a bit shocked over her actions. I figured that she would be back in a little while, but that didn't happen. The next thing that did happen was alarming.

Once she left, Bree came in and plopped her 10-year-old behind on the counter. She had tears streaming down her face, and I tried to tell her that it was just a little argument and that Mom would be back in a little while. The next words out of her mouth ambushed me.

"Dad, you don't know what it's like when you are not here. All she does is yell at us and lay on the couch. She is mean and I can't take it anymore," she said. It would seem that my children had noticed the change in Anna as well, but what was disturbing was that she had not just started acting aggressive and unusual toward me, she was also that way toward the kids. Obviously, it was very upsetting to them as well. I felt that it was time for action.

It was right about this time that Andrea Yates drowned all five of her children in Texas. The media reported across America that Andrea Yates was bipolar. The story was horrifying to me. I surmised that she and Anna had similar diagnoses. At the time of these tragic murders, the media also reported that Andrea was taking Effexor and Remeron, both anti-depressants, and had been previously taking Welbutrin, as well as Haldol. Anna had taken Effexor and Welbutrin, too. In my messed-up, unrealistic world, I began to draw a conclusion that was not true.

The truth was later reported that Andrea Yates' mental instability was due to postpartum depression and complicated by severe psychosis. In all actuality, Andrea Yates and Anna had very little in common. With that being said, Anna did not return home. She took herself back to the hospital. This was actually the correct thing for her to do, but I didn't see it that way.

The following Monday morning, I was at the county courthouse filing for a restraining order against my wife of nearly fourteen years and the mother of my children. I also began taking the necessary steps to file for a divorce. I was in a panic, and I was trying to make the horrible situation go away. Since it did not get better and go away by itself, I jumped into action to make it happen. I met with lawyers and paralegals and made phone calls like there was no tomorrow. I was a man with a plan on a mission. I figured that enough was enough and I would take control of my life. I had resolve, I had purpose, and I finally had control of my life again. It should have felt incredibly good to finally see some sort of an end to what was the main ingredient of my troublesome life. I should have had some feeling of hope and peace, but I did not. I did not feel any better, nor did I feel any hope, and with no hope, there was no peace. Still, I dragged myself forward, holding on to the idea that divorcing Anna was the answer. I was fighting for air and gasping for breath. Not for one single second did I feel good about what I was doing. Notice I said, "What I was doing."

This is the part of the story where I am forced to admit that I was the total schmuck. I didn't even give Anna a chance. She tried to talk to me and I would just hang up on her. That person I used to be, the person who sided with grace and forgiveness just a few years earlier, was lost in the anger, panic and bitterness. I simply refused to talk to her. The one thing that we always could do was talk it out, but I refused to talk.

The divorce papers were served on Anna in the hospital. As I wrote that last sentence, I wanted to kick my own butt for being so heartless. I know, I know… I was such a jerk! But that is what happened. She called me in tears, and I did what any husband who has just served his wife with divorce papers would do. I slammed the phone down. I did this not because I hated her, or was angry with her. I did it because I wanted to be free from her situation. I was spent. I could not deal with her. I wanted out. Truth be told, I wanted a divorce from her illness, not from Anna. With fear, panic and bitterness whispering in my ear, I stood firm in my decision to get a divorce.

It hit me one afternoon that I had to tell my children that I had made the decision to divorce their Mom. This will go down in history as the single most difficult thing I have ever had to do. Bree and Aaron sat on the couch and Bekah was sitting next to me. I thought that it would be best to come straight to the point, so I just said it.

"Daddy has made a decision to get a divorce from Mommy." This was not one of my more eloquent moments. They just stared at me and said nothing. Then I continued, "I think that it is best for us at this time." Blank stares again.

"So, what do you think?" I asked, hoping for any response at all.

Aaron was the first to speak. "Will we ever see Mom again?"

"Of course. This is between me and Mommy, and you will see her all the time. I do not want you to be separated from her. She is your Mom, and she will always be your Mom."

As I answered that question, I wondered what the hell I was doing. It just felt wrong. Still, I would not just call the whole thing off.

"Well, at least I will be like my friend Eli. His Mom is divorced," Rebekah said with a smile on her face that said, "I am not okay with this, but I will make the best of it."

Bree just wanted to know the plans and vital statistics of what was next – living arrangements, who was getting what car and if she would have to change schools. I hated every single minute of that conversation. It felt so wrong. Between Aaron's worry about seeing his Mom again and Rebekah's smile of denial, I was dying inside.

Later that night, Anna called and practically begged me to talk to her. All she wanted was a chance to explain and figure out how we could fix it. I refused again. I hung up the phone while she was in mid-sentence. I got a phone call from her friend on a Saturday morning. She was coming to pick up Anna's belongings. This meant that Anna had finally come to grips with things and was moving on. This was a good thing, I thought. Later that day, her friend came and cleaned out Anna's side of the closet, and within an hour, Anna was out of our home.

That same day, I took down the wedding pictures and every other picture that had Anna and me in it. I took them outside and threw them in the dumpster. Thirty minutes later, guess who was in the dumpster digging out the pictures? Yes, the idiot who threw them away was now digging through rotting garbage to get his memories back. I was really sold on divorce wasn't I? I was not just an idiotic jerk lunatic; I was now a dumpster-diving idiotic jerk lunatic.

I had plenty of support in this decision. Co-workers, friends and neighbors didn't blame me one bit. They made me feel justified in my actions for short periods of time. Family, however, was quite a different story. I found that my family supported me, but in a peculiar way that did not exactly support my decision.

My Mom said a lot of things to me during that time. Most of her advice came completely unsolicited, but mothers get a free pass in the "mind your own business" category. No matter what she said, she ended every paragraph with, "But it's your decision." My sister just kept asking me, "So what are you going to do?" It didn't matter that I told her a hundred times that I was filing for divorce, she would still ask. This was her way of asking me if I was sure about what I was doing without being disagreeable, which I found funny. Nothing else had ever stopped her from being disagreeable with me before.

My dad, on the other hand, said close to nothing to me. It was not that he didn't care; it was because he did care. We have never talked much about it, but I would bet that he had his reservations about me getting a divorce. He was the guy that taught me the importance of commitment and sticking with a person. His lack of opinion was deafening. He just kept saying, "Be sure you know what you are doing."

One night, I got a call from the hospital that informed me that Anna was getting discharged from the hospital and they needed to know if she had a safe place to go.

"I don't know where she will go, but she can't come here," I said.

And the heartless bastard award goes to… me.

I sat down on the bed and began to sob. I was sticking to my guns, boy, doing the right thing. Holding strong. But what if it was the wrong thing? I lay back on the bed and just wept. Breanna came in and crawled up next to me and lay down in the same position. She rested her arm across my chest and profoundly declared, "Sucks, huh?"

"Yeah, it does," I said between my pathetic hyperventilating.

"It will be alright. You always do the right thing."

I had no idea what I was doing, and if a "right thing" existed, I had no idea what it was. Bree just laid there for a while until we were both laughing. Soon enough, Aaron and Bekah came in and we were all goofing off, wrestling on the bed. It felt good to have a little fun, but I couldn't help but feel a void. Anna was not there and without her being there, we just were not complete. I was beginning to drown in my despair.

I am from San Diego, California, so water safety is something that I learned at a young age, especially because I spent a lot of time at Mission Beach as a teenager. Watching lifeguards rescue people all day long is something I got used to, but I never got used to witnessing the rescue attempts that failed.

On a warm, beautiful summer day, a group of friends and I took a trip to the beach. We met with another group of kids from a completely different part of town. The two groups hit it off from the start and spent all day sharing each other's sodas, chips and boogie-boards. It was one of the most memorable times at the beach that summer because we had found new friends. That was the day we witnessed one of our new friends drown.

It happened just as the sun was getting low on the horizon and the lifeguards were getting ready to call it a day and go home. Three die-hards were still in the water and the rest of us had settled into our dry clothes and were preparing for the evening bonfire. Then, without any notice, two of the lifeguards sped past us, kicking sand in their wake. We could see our three diehard, boogie-boarding friends swimming frantically in the water. Two were swimming together and one was just frantically splashing about. They were in the middle of a riptide, and the severe undertow was pulling our new friend April into the sea. The two veteran surfers knew what to do and immediately began to save themselves by swimming along the shore to get away from the fierce current. This was April's first beach excursion. She was a native of Colorado and had only lived in San Diego for just three months. She did not know what to do in case of a riptide. She had no idea what was happening to her. The two veterans just sprang into action out of reflex and assumed that April knew what to do. It was like the ocean was picking on the new kid.

Just as the two lifeguards hit the water, April was engulfed by a wave. It consumed her, and then she was gone. The lifeguards shot through the water in her direction.

One second… two seconds… three seconds and April did not re-surface.

We all began to move toward the water to get a closer look, and then panic set in as someone in the crowd yelled, "She is going to drown!"

Fifteen seconds… sixteen seconds… the lifeguards dove under the water searching for her. Two more lifeguards appeared to assist in the desperate search.

Twenty seconds… thirty seconds… still no April. One minute… two minutes… still no April. Then about fifteen yards to the north and fifty yards out from the original spot, April emerged safely in the hands of a female lifeguard who was pulling her toward the shore.

The scene on the shore was like watching a movie. We watched lifeguards, paramedics and police personnel scramble to bring April back to life. She just lay there, limp, wet and a little blue. I knew she was dead. Then the paramedics started CPR. I remember the first compression on her chest and seawater spurting out of her mouth. I turned away as did a couple of others. The girl next to me, April's friend, was in tears. All of us were. The two veteran surfers tried to explain that they didn't know that she didn't know what to do and that they didn't know that she was inexperienced. "I told her not to go out too far," said her friend. Then we heard the paramedic yell, "Clear, clear, clear!" We turned to see the paramedic zap April's chest with electricity. Her body jumped. "Clear!" *Zap!* "C'mon Damn it!" he yelled, just like in the movies. "Clear!"

April coughed a few seconds later. The crowd cheered, and we, her friends and new friends, breathed again ourselves. April was taken to the hospital. We never saw her again, or any of our new friends from across town. It was a big day for April. She had waded out into troubled waters, the water had tried to kill her, she had drowned and she had died. For reasons unknown to any of us, she was revived and lived to tell about it. Metaphorically, the same thing happened to me twenty-five years later.

CHAPTER 24

V-fib

V-fib (ventricular fibrillation) is a condition in which there is uncoordinated contraction of the cardiac muscles of the ventricles of the heart. As a result, the heart fails to adequately pump blood and hypoxia (a condition in which the body as a whole is deprived of adequate oxygen supply) will occur, followed by unconsciousness within twenty to thirty seconds. Then you die.

V-fib is the only way to describe me at this time. I was in emotional as well as spiritual v-fib. I was having my near-death experience, just like April. I cannot adequately explain the serious, self-destructive path I was traveling. I was smoking two packs a day, drinking constantly, angry, inward, mean, and hopeless. In no way was I in a mental or emotional state that would allow me to make fair and good decisions. I was a mess.

I was getting ready to divorce my wife, split our home and bring my children undue pain. In trying to protect myself and survive, I was doing the opposite and simply killing myself in the process. Mental hypoxia was choking me out. I needed someone to yell, "*Clear!*" and zap me one.

As it turns out, that is exactly what happened. God dialed 911, and he sent some very unlikely paramedics to zap me. I called to talk to my good friend, Stephen, on a Saturday night. Stephen and his wife Kendra had been on my volunteer staff at First Church when we were dismissed. I told him that I was getting a divorce. He spent thirty minutes trying to explain to me that I was making a mistake. I hung up feeling frustrated with him because he was more on Anna's side than mine.

It surprised me when Stephen was knocking on my front door at 6 a.m. the next morning. He had to get up at 4 a.m. to drive to San Diego. That's a good friend. We spent all morning talking, and then he said something that was overwhelming. He said, "You can't divorce Anna."

…One second… two seconds… I didn't respond.

"There has to be Rudy and Anna. There just has to be."

…Twenty seconds… thirty seconds… still no response.

"There can't be a Rudy without an Anna and there can't be an Anna without a Rudy."

Clear… zap!

My son Aaron was around eight years old at the time. We were talking about the divorce and he asked me point-blank, "Dad, why are you getting a divorce anyway?" I gave him my answer and he did not like it. "If you divorce Mom, you will regret it for the rest of your life," he said.

Clear… zap!

The guilt was unbearable. I was doing something that I really didn't want to do. I had gotten myself in the middle of something that I couldn't get out of, and so I pressed forward. Stephen and Aaron were the first two "common-sense paramedics" that began the process of reviving my sensibility, but in the end, it could only be me. I had to make the choice to accept my mistake and get my wife back.

Anna did not have a place to go when she was released from the hospital. I left her no choice but to go and live at a women's half-way house called Big Sisters. If I wasn't riddled by guilt before, I certainly was now. With me being crazy and unrealistic, Anna with all her issues still managed to make the best out of the situation. She still went to her daily meetings at the hospital and learned the bus routes to get around. She was doing better than I was. She had hired an attorney with the help of her brothers and was ready to face whatever came next in the divorce proceedings. She told her brothers that she couldn't believe that I wouldn't talk to her. She told them that the one thing that we could always do was talk things out. I was not willing until the day I met up with her face to face.

I got a call from Anna's brother because he needed to come and get some paperwork for her. I decided to take it to her myself. The following day after work, I drove to the Big Sister's House in Hillcrest, San Diego. I called Anna to let her know that I was coming. She already knew because her brother had told her. The drive was very rough. I was nervous and didn't know what to expect. I knew that I had been a complete idiot, and in most of the world's eyes, I was a total fool. I didn't know what to expect. Would I knock on the door and get jumped by a team of women from the big sisterhood? I was scared of what was going to happen. Anna was not a person I feared, but you know what they say: "Hell hath no fury like a woman scorned."

I pulled up in front of the house and there, on the front steps, sat Anna. I didn't want to admit it, but I was so glad to see her. My heart raced with that same feeling I had when she walked down the aisle on our wedding day. My body yearned for any type of embrace from her. The feeling of connection was astounding. There was my wife, my friend, my partner. I was such a fool. Something inside me began to break down.

...Clear... zap!

Anna walked up and tried to just have me hand her the paperwork through the small opening in the passenger side window. I opened the door and got out of my truck. I walked over to her and handed her the papers.

"It would be ridiculous to act this way. Can we talk?" She agreed to talk and we sat on the steps. I updated her on the kids' grades, activities and all the gossip in the apartment complex. We talked and laughed for nearly two hours. Finally, Anna said to me, "I don't get this. We can always talk, and here we are talking and laughing, so what's the deal here?"

She was so dead right. I knew in that moment what I had to do. I was doing a stupid thing and I needed to stop.

...Clear... zap! Beep...beep... beep...

I was revived and my sensibility and my heart began to function again. We made plans to meet at a park the following weekend so she could see the kids. We directly violated the restraining order and didn't care. We played with the kids and had a little lunch. It was then that I learned that the weekend Anna had walked out; she was in the middle of a medication change. Normally she would have been admitted to the hospital so that things like this could be avoided. When a person gets off a medication or is introduced to a new med, this is standard procedure. It could have all been avoided, and it was her doctor's indiscretion that caused this whole event. No, he didn't make me file for divorce, but it could have been so much easier if the med change had been handled properly. Now, with her meds adjusted, Anna was doing really well.

A week later, we had coffee at Starbucks. I brought a list of things I wanted to have happen, and she had a list as well. The lists matched perfectly. Anna came back home the following weekend.

Once again, God saved me from myself and our family remained intact. We came so close to losing everything that was so important to us. It was God who did the saving, because normally people don't survive these types of things without Him. Was I praying for God to intervene and save this marriage and this family? No, I was not. Believe it or not, Anna was. It was the love and grace of God at work in my life again, and I still didn't see it.

CHAPTER 25

Commonsensical Insanity

You know, it is true that you don't really appreciate what you have got until it is in jeopardy of being taken from you. I had just about single-handedly ended our marriage and family. Our family is now my most precious and valuable possession.

We had a lot to work through afterward. Anna felt betrayed and abandoned by me, and for good reasons. I had good reasons for my actions as well, but the bottom line was that it was not the right thing to do. I did get my head back on straight. I took responsibility for my actions and I went back to see the manly-man counselor. We discussed anger, resentment, and all that good stuff, and I was able to recover from panic attacks, fear and anger. I still had the same old resentment and bitterness, and now it had seeped out toward not just the few people that actually hurt me, but the entire church and its people. The bitterness was spreading like a cancer and it was eating me alive. I just could not find the strength or will to just let it go.

I knew that I was not healthy emotionally or spiritually, but at the very least, I was able to salvage my family and my relationship with Anna. I guess this would be a good time to mention that we had pretty much stopped going to church. Anna didn't care, and I didn't want to, so we didn't go. We tried going to a church right down the street from where we lived, but Anna and I decided that we didn't like it. The kids managed to get involved in that church without us. I forbade my kids to tell anyone what my past was and that I was a pastor. I'd just drop them off for youth events, small group meetings and retreats. I had become the parent that I used to like to talk about. I was now the non-committed Christian.

Anna and I just attended every now and then. I hated to go mainly because I just thought the whole place was full of phonies and that if given the chance, they would take my legs out from under me. I chose not to talk to anyone. It was safer that way. The other reason I didn't like to go was because I couldn't go without a cigarette for a whole hour.

One Sunday morning, the pastor made his plea for people to come forward and give their lives to Jesus. Usually Anna and I left because we could avoid the crowd and no one would talk to us. This particular Sunday morning, just as we were about to leave, the pastor said, "There is a former pastor here. He has been hurt, lied about, and has left the ministry. You are at a place to find hope." Well if that wasn't the strangest thing. "That guy is reading my mail," I thought.

I waited around until the end and let some people clear out. I went to the front and introduced myself to the pastor, saying, "Hello, I'm the pastor you were talking about." We talked for a few moments and we set up a time to talk. We met at Starbucks and I told him about everything that had happened. He seemed genuinely concerned and told me about the church and how I'd like it. He took my number and said he'd check in on me from time to time. I left feeling good about things, and I thought that perhaps I had come to the right place. I tried to go to church regularly and get back in the game. I did not stay consistent, and I fell away in a short period of time. I never did get a phone call from him.

Funny thing is, I ran into the pastor in the foyer one Sunday morning. He didn't even remember who I was. It didn't bother me. I was used to leaders who pretended to care. I just went out to the parking lot for a smoke. I remember standing next to my car with a Camel in my mouth. A church parking attendant drove up in his golf cart and told me that I was not allowed to smoke on the property. I asked him if he had health insurance. He asked me why I wanted to know, and I said, "Because if you don't get the <bleep> away from me, you are going to need it!" Did you know that a golf cart can burn rubber? His golf cart did!

I am not particularly proud of moments like that, but sometimes it's just nice to be reminded that I am, after all, human. Besides, stories like this humor me.

One of the good things that came out of all this was that I got to know who I was. I mean, I really came to know myself. It started when I admitted that I was making a mistake by divorcing Anna. My good friend Barry always asks, "What are you thinking when you go to bed at night?" That is the time when we are alone with our thoughts and we can clearly evaluate who we are and what we are about. It is like looking in a mirror that shows us the goods we don't really want to see.

What I was thinking about and what I saw in the mirror was an incomplete and broken person. By broken I do not mean a person that had felt great sadness and is learning from his mistakes. I mean broken in the way that you throw a cell phone against the wall and it shatters into a million pieces. I was broken as in not working properly.

Things had always been sort of automatic with me. I just made things happen by sheer will. I am very strong-willed and naturally aggressive. I saw myself as an in-control kind of guy and believed that I was a force to be reckoned with. My life situation had challenged all of that, and sheer will and aggressiveness were getting the snot kicked out of them by the new kid on the block – adversity.

Adversity is a worthy opponent and will beat you every time by simple, steady, continuous and repetitive blows. It is not adversity's goal to beat you with one swift knockout, but to slowly beat you into submission and cause as much agony in your defeat as possible.

This was new for me. I had always won, always controlled, always overcome. Not this time. Adversity had me in a headlock, holding a mirror to my face, saying, "This is who you really are. You are not who you think you are." I was stripped of all my pride. I was reduced to a man led by fear, self-doubt and remorse. I was pinned against the ropes and adversity was working me over. I started to give in by settling for the easy answers like smoking, booze and thinking that divorce was going to solve my problems. It scared me that I had re-treated to what I thought was a safe and trouble-free place.

Mirrors don't lie. I did not like who I saw in that mirror. The true measure of a man is who he is when faced with adversity, and I was coming up short. This did not happen to me in an instant. I didn't just change from being a man of insight and resolve because I went through one difficult situation. I was and still am a tough customer. I am all the good things that I mentioned and even more. Above all else, I am a survivor. But when I went through all of these terrible events of life, it slowly, and I mean it was *slow*, convinced me that I was not the person I thought I was.

If you let it, adversity will strip you of all your pride, all of your self-worth. It is a liar that will talk you into thinking the wrong ideas are right and the right ideas are wrong. Like smoking and drinking to hide the pain, even abandoning your spouse of fourteen years, or throwing up your hands and quitting. Adversity wants to keep hitting you with blow after blow and trick you into following that fear, self-doubt and remorse. Once you do this, turn off the lights, the party is over. You're done.

I came to a crossroads. It was not a place of healing, but it was a place of resolve. I knew enough of myself to realize that I was not behaving in a manner that was historically consistent with who I was. I reached a place that was more common sense than a true place of restoration.

I decided to stop getting worked over and fight. That was the common sense. I needed to take my life back and protect the things that were truly important to me – my wife, my kids, and of course, myself. I was tired of feeling like a victim. Adversity had a grip on me, but I came back swinging, and swinging hard. What was not so healthy was my resolve not to let anyone or anything get in my way, hurt me, or make me feel bad about myself again. I had a chip on my shoulder and dared anyone to knock it off. I went a little far with that attitude and that was insane. This is what I call the place of commonsensical insanity.

Okay, it's no secret, I am not the nicest person at times, but with my newfound attitude, it was ridiculous. This is why I was threatening a parking lot attendant in a church parking lot.

CHAPTER 26

"And they lived happily ever after—
Hang onto your butts, here we go again!"

Normalcy came home with Anna. We had a short time of Mom at home and dad going to work. We were like any great television family: The Bradys, Cleavers, Waltons or the Huxtables. It was great.

Anna was able to go trick-or-treating with the kids and was home for Thanksgiving. She did very well for a while. It was not uncommon for her to come home and function well for a while. I would sometimes even think that she was finally recovered and would beat the depression and manage the bipolar and BPD. I was fooled every time.

Christmas rounded the corner and Anna was back in the hospital. This, of course, was not uncommon; it was the holidays which led to a trip back to the funny farm.

Just when I thought that we were getting to the "…and they lived happily ever after" part, I'd get a surprise ending. It was not easy on the kids, but this being trip number fifty-something, they were a bit calloused and unaffected by this trip back. When the kids came home and I informed them that Mom was in the hospital again, my son responded with, "Hang onto your butts, here we go again!"

Over the next year and a half, things only got worse. Anna made three suicide attempts. This was when she tried to hang herself and tried to overdose twice. The hanging was quite horrific to me. The attempt was made with bed sheets and sprinkler pipe in her room while admitted to the hospital. She tried to block the door to her room with a mattress and made a rope out of bed sheets with a loop at the end as a makeshift noose. Thankfully, the hospital had a camera and a window to the room, and an orderly was able to muscle his way through before she actually got the sheet around her neck. She usually made the attempts at the hospital because Anna's greatest fear was not dying; it was having me or the kids find her dead. So, being considerate and all, she made her attempts away from us.

She tried to overdose when she was once again on a walk and swallowed a bottle of pills. She called a hotline from the parking lot of the DMV to find out how long it was going to take her to die. The hotline personnel called an ambulance. Upon arriving to the emergency room, Anna called me.

When she told me where she was, I was angry. As I said earlier, I do not get suicide. I find the idea foreign and unrealistic. The very idea of Anna wanting to permanently take herself away from me and the kids was absurd and selfish. I had had enough, and I made sure that she knew how I felt. I was infuriated when she laughed at me and made light of the situation. When she made jokes about the placement of the heart monitor sensors on her female anatomy, I wanted to drive to the hospital and smack her.

That is why I got great pleasure out of hearing how disgusted she was when they forced the charcoal mixture down her throat. I would have shoved Kingsford Briquettes down her throat if I had been given half a chance. No, I was not nice to her when she would attempt suicide. To me, she was just giving up, and I knew that she had so much more to offer the world.

The second time Anna tried to overdose was in the hospital, and she once again tried to take a handful of pills. This time was well-planned out and calculated. She cheeked her medication and collected the pills in a paper napkin hidden in a drawer. When she figured she had enough to kill herself, she took them all at once and waited for the pills to do their job. This did not result in death, but in having her stomach pumped. There's nothing like getting a tube shoved down the pie-hole, all the way to the stomach, and switching on the vacuum. I'm sure the medical profession has a cleaner and more suitable description, but it is the equivalent of having the hose of a Shop-Vac snaked into your gut and then having the switch flipped. She didn't like that either, and I once again, relished the thought.

Taking joy in my wife's misery when it came to the charcoal and wanting to shove briquettes into her mouth was not a mature response. I know this. It was how I felt, and it was infuriating to me that she would actually believe that the kids and I wanted her to go away so we would be better off.

People have often made comments to me like, "She put you through hell." I don't really think that way. It is more like we went through hell together. Anna didn't set out to make me suffer some grievous life. She would have changed it all if she could have. She believed that if she killed herself, the kids and I would be better off. It was her solution to an ugly situation.

We battled Anna's unhealthy thought processes for the next three years. There was definitely stress in our relationship, but it was not because of relational differences. Our stress was because she was not recovering. I am not sure who wanted her freedom from her illness more. She was tired of feeling bad, and the storm was chasing her down every day.

"The Storm" is how Anna describes the onslaught of depression. She describes it as a dark cloud creeping up on her, and if she doesn't run, it will catch her and pour out the black rain of hopelessness that is depression's dark friend. Anna spent most of the days running from the rain. I couldn't even offer as much as a simple umbrella. I felt as useless as I did helpless. The storm sucks.

I wanted so badly to protect her from the downpour of suicidal thoughts and self-loathing, which was in our life far too often. I began to be less frustrated with Anna and became more of a contributor of hope. Yes, I was still frustrated with the illness, but I made a decision to focus my frustrations on the illness and not on the person with the illness. I finally learned. I finally had a little empathy. I finally understood.

I had thought that depression was a load of crap. I had thought that a person could just shake it off and make it go away. I was of a school of thought that believed that a person can just wish or will depression away. I had also believed that if a person suffering from depression did not just will it away, they were just seeking attention and chose to be that way. Depression is not a choice. It is an illness. It is a storm. It is a drowning rain of hopelessness.

What makes a person want to cut, burn or bloody herself? What makes a person want to die and leave her babies alone without a Mommy to kiss their owies? What will make a person think that her family is better off without her? How can a Mom or dad rationalize that missing his or her child's first step, piece of artwork hanging on the refrigerator, a sixteenth birthday, graduation or wedding day is for the best? Why would a person exchange that joy for a premature casket?

Why would anyone choose death over life? It is because of the storm, it is because of the black rain of the hopelessness. Because of depression, that's why. All I had to do now was find the correct foul-weather gear. I realized that Anna's victory over the storm was not going to happen by running from or avoiding the storm. She needed to learn how to weather the storm.

When we lived in the south, we got to experience the infamous tornado warning. I am a native Californian, and I have felt my fair share of tremors and earthquakes. I was pretty close to the Northridge quake of 1994 when it rocked my house at 4:30 a.m. I am not foreign to natural disasters. I will confess that earthquakes do not scare me like a tornado does. My fear of tornados is not even in the same zip code as quakes.

When we experienced our first tornado warning, it sealed the fear in me. It was a stormy night and I was up watching the weather reports on television. The weatherman had already said that we were on a tornado watch. Anna was already scared of the idea of a tornado striking, so I had the news watch duty.

The local weatherman was up all night watching the storm and reporting every fifteen minutes or so. He interrupted my show for about the tenth time, and he announced in a calm but urgent voice that, "rotation in the storm has been spotted over the county." What did that mean? It meant that a *tor-frigg'n-nado* was coming! As the words left his mouth, I heard hell open up and scream!

The tornado siren went off with its deafening screech. No one told me that the siren was exactly twelve feet from my back yard, and the howling siren sent me into a panic of epic proportions. I ran to the bedroom where Anna was still asleep. I couldn't have that, so I woke her up. Her eyes opened to the sound of hell's screams.

"What is it?" she asked, leaping out of bed.

"A tornado, can't you hear?" If I could have screamed, I would have… like an 8-year-old girl!

Anna took off running down the hall, calling on the name of Jesus.

I ran behind her, praying, "What she said, Lord! What she said!"

She headed to the kids' bedrooms.

"What are you doing?" I asked, grabbing her hand to stop her.

"I am getting the kids," she said in a panic.

"Wait, let's see what everyone else is doing."

I went to the front window to see what the rest of the world was doing. There wasn't even as much as a light on – not one light in one house. No one cared about the warning. No one even got out of bed. Within ten minutes, it was over and the weatherman called off the warning. We learned later that we lived in Tornado Alley, but a tornado had not touched down in our county in twenty years. No one worried about tornados there. No one cared about the siren because no one feared storms or the tornados. Our lives were not like that. We feared the next storm of depression. For us, a storm was always on Anna's horizon.

She knows the signs and she knows when it is coming. I began to see the signs as well, and soon I could forecast the next day's emotional weather for her. My sister had a calendar marked up from the previous years, and we learned that Anna had a pattern that cycled annually. With this information, all we really could do was prepare for the storm. There is about as much we can do to prevent it as the Weather Channel can do to prevent an earthquake or tornado from happening.

We accepted it as part of life, much like we accept the changes in weather. Some days are sunny, some are cloudy. Some days bring severe weather, and other days are blue skies and cool breezes. We can accept it, but we don't have to fear drowning because of a few raindrops.

Anna didn't see that she needed to weather the storm. All she saw was that it was coming and its arrival meant feelings of hopelessness that were going to be so severe that she would feel like dying. The fear of depression itself made her depressed.

Weathering the storm of depression takes a lot of work by the individual suffering with depression. It requires that person to be downright selfish if they want to get better. This was not an easy concept for me to accept. Anna's world had to revolve around herself, and that meant she had to ignore everyone else if need be. This was not an easy concept for Anna to get her head around, either. Before the depression won out, her world revolved around her family and her children. Everything she did was for them. Now she had to put herself first and if she didn't, everyone involved would suffer.

CHAPTER 27

Hope: take daily as needed for pain

Anna has had many doctors and therapists over the years. I nicknamed them all so as to point out their eccentricities and oddities. None of them were quite Frasier Crane, my favorite TV shrink, but all of them had a distinct quality that either made them help or hurt her recovery.

Anna's first psychologist, the one I called Dr. Kindergarten, set the bar a little low when it came to mental health professionals. I would describe him as "good enough," and he did get Anna set straight for the time being back in 1996. He was not very in-tune with the needs to a family who was dealing with a person with mental illness.

By 2000, we were introduced to several other mental health professionals. I need to point out that all but a couple were helpful, personable and genuinely cared about Anna and our family's survival. The most interesting and humorous part of this story is that all but one of these mental health professionals were of Jewish descent. There were more "steins" and "burgs" in her medical chart than you can imagine. I referred to them as the Hebrew Mental Mafia.

Dr. "Funky" was the doctor that discovered and diagnosed Anna with BPD. He was a hilarious little man with a sharp intellect and a heart of gold. To emphasize a point, he did not raise his voice, he lowered it. His deep, rich voice would drop to a lower octave and then whisper to drive home the point he wanted to make.

"Golf Course" was my least favorite doctor. This was the doctor who always made it clear with his attitude that he'd rather golf than be at work. Okay, that isn't so bad, I guess. Most of us would rather be doing something other than working. I just think that telling the husband of one of his patients to "please hurry with your question; I have a 2:30 tee time," is not very professional. He was quick with his prescription pad, too. I think that he was the one that had Anna on eight different medications at once. He also once told me that it would be completely inappropriate to talk to me in private about my wife. He was the only doctor that refused to talk to me.

An outside program assigned Anna a therapist. This program was to care for people who may need additional help with day-to-day life. Most of these therapists went to the patients' homes and spent time with them. Often they would pick patients up, drive them to their appointments and support them with whatever they may need, even help people with the day-to-day needs in their home. Not Anna's therapist. She insisted that Anna drive to Einstein Bros. Bagels and meet her there. The place was nearly a thirty-minute drive for Anna. The therapist would do whatever was convenient for her and not for Anna. If Anna did not agree with her, this "professional" would argue with Anna and send her home in worse shape than she was in the first place. I referred to her as "The Bagel-Broad." Anna eventually dismissed her and discontinued that program.

"Sweetness" was a nurse on the third floor who did nothing but keep Anna focused on hope. She was sweet, but tough. She didn't take the self-destructive talk of patients and she would nail them for it. Then, in her sweet-tough way, she would give a person hope, help and freedom. I loved her. She was the first mental health professional that gave me hope. She would tell me to hang in there and that one day I'd see a better Anna. I hung on to those words for years. She eventually had to quit her job because this sweet lady was having her own battle with depression. I was deeply saddened when she was no longer there.

I can go on and on about the good, the bad and the ugly of mental health workers. There were ones that would take things personally, get into petty fights with the patients and use their power to punish the disagreeable and unacceptable mental patients. It is as absurd as it sounds. This happened to Anna a few times, and if you know me at all, you know that a few times I had hospital administrators standing at attention at their own desks, apologizing. As a result of my involvement, I got to see a few of those people removed from either their positions or their jobs altogether.

Many professionals did amazingly with Anna – too many to remember and too many to mention. Of all the wonderful people that worked with Anna and me in this quest toward healing, two people in particular stand out – a therapist named Judy and a psychiatrist called Marc. These individuals took it upon themselves to go the extra mile for my wife. Without their undying devotion to their craft, Anna would probably be in a hospital somewhere, or even worse, she may no longer be alive. I can in no way tell this story without including the efforts of these two people who delivered hope.

If angels were therapists, Judy would have wings. I only had the pleasure of meeting her a couple of times, but each time was like sitting down to tea with a family member. I am not really sure how to describe her, but I just thought she was very cool.

Anna and Judy developed a tight bond, and their friendship was something they both protected. I was so impressed with Judy that I tried to see her for therapy. Judy refused. She thought it might interfere with what was going on with Anna in their sessions. Yes, a therapist was rejecting me and choosing my wife over me, but it was the wise thing to do. I wasn't nearly as hurt as I pretended to be. It was fun to make Judy squirm a little as I reminded her that she rejected me. She was a good sport, played along, and reminded me how insignificant I was in comparison to Anna.

I think that the most effective therapy for Anna was Judy's commitment and support to her. I am not sure what happened in those sessions. Anna was not always eager to share. But the results were invaluable to her recovery. Thankful does not accurately describe my feelings for Judy.

"He is the meanest little bastard I have ever met! I hate him!" That was how Anna described to me a new doctor on weekend rounds that had just placed her back in ICU.

"I hate that little Nazi! He is just out to get me and I did nothing!" It would seem that my mentally ill wife had done something against the rules again, and she was back in ICU. She was demanding that I come break her out of the hospital, and she wanted me to "kick the crap out of" a new doctor that put her there. I knew better than to over-react since I knew that she had probably done something to put her safety in jeopardy. I was right.

"Cheeking" meds was against the rules, and as it turns out, she had a collection of pills that she was planning on downing that weekend. In other words, she was planning her suicide. This new doctor had done the correct thing by placing her in the ICU under suicide watch. The "new" doctor was actually a director of psychiatry at this hospital. He was a veteran.

What angered Anna so badly was that he knew her game. It was game, set and match. Anna didn't have a prayer with this guy. What she didn't know was that the only way to win this game was to lose to Marc. She had to bow to him and let him help, listen to him and stop the acting out. Marc was a master at her game.

Marc was a thin man of medium height, somewhere in his fifties. He had salt and pepper hair, wore reading glasses and hated cold rooms. His face seldom wore a smile, but he didn't frown. I was neither impressed nor unimpressed. I think the feeling was mutual. What I didn't know was that inside this small, Jewish man was a blazing fire. He would turn out to be a blast of fury when crossed, and this infused with his passion for his patients made him a superhero in my eyes.

On the Monday following the incident with Anna's re-admission to ICU, she was allowed to return to the third floor where she could have some of her freedoms back. It was during this time that she was having the E.C.T. procedure. She was scheduled to have her next treatment the following Tuesday. It was only during this treatment that she realized that Marc was the E.C.T. doctor. Marc was actually the doctor that was in charge of all E.C.T. procedures at the hospital. This sent Anna into orbit. She railed at Marc, verbally attacking him. She called him everything she could think of, including Hitler. She insulted the size of his manhood, his race and his integrity. She later told me that all Marc did was laugh.

Week after week, she saw Marc three times a week during E.C.T. treatment and every other weekend if Marc was on call. She was not a big fan of Marc. He was stubborn and direct, and his demeanor was stern. Each and every time Anna saw him, she would call me with an unfavorable report. He was a jerk, he was an idiot, he was mean, he was too angry… blab blab blab.

I got to where I would wait for her to see him. He may have been mean and a jerk, but what I saw from the outside looking in was that he was breaking through. Marc was making headway and I loved it. It didn't take too terribly long for the reports to change from, "I saw the jerk today," to a much more favorable, "I was talking to Marc today, and he said…" She had a more favorable view of Marc, but she still was no fan of Marc's moods or methods. They still argued, and he just pissed Anna off so badly that she would scream – at me! I didn't like him much for that, but she was feeling an emotion other than guilt, shame or hurt. She would tell me things like, "I'm not going to give Marc the satisfaction of knowing that he did so-and-so."

"He isn't going to be able to tell me 'I told you so.'"

"I am going to show him!"

Marc was teaching her to lose the game and by doing so, Anna was taking her first steps toward winning the battle. The last thing that I ever thought would happen was the day that Marc came to Anna and asked her if she wanted him to be her doctor.

"Your doctor is retiring and I don't take new patients, but I will take you if you want to have me as a doctor," he said. That took Anna completely off guard.

"I will need to think about that, Marc."

"Well, discuss it with your husband and let me know." With that, he left her to make her decision.

My first reaction to this was negative. I didn't want to have my life bombarded with listening to my wife's complaining about her psychiatrist and their love/hate relationship. In the end, I gave into the right thing to do, which was letting her make the decision herself. Besides that, I had seen the marked improvement in Anna's ability to react like an adult to her situation and not like a 13-year-old brat. As it turned out, she decided to make Marc her official doctor, and it proved to be just what the doctor ordered.

The relationship between Marc and Anna was that of prize fighters in a boxing ring. It was a constant battle. In secret, I cheered for Marc. It was not difficult to see what his plan was. Never give Anna the upper hand, never give in and never give up. He never did.

There is no way I can explain the positively pain-in-the-proverbial-butt Anna was during this time. She was argumentative, stubborn, defensive, adversarial, sarcastic, moody, and at times, just plain volatile. She was not easy to take, and let one thing not go the way she thought it should go and *boom!* Conflict! I also need to point out that Marc was her doctor during all of her antics and attempts. She had to face him when she acted out.

Marc was a pain to Anna as well. He was wise, poignant, direct, and just as volatile. He was not afraid of an argument and he never backed down. He was like a bulldog on a turkey leg. In a word, he was relentless. I had the opportunity to sit in on a couple of their encounters. Yes, encounters. These were not sessions, or appointments, they were encounters – close encounters with dramatic results.

Once, Anna had stolen a pin from a bulletin board and used it to scratch her arms up. Of course, she was caught and thrown back into ICU. The next day, Marc walked into the room, threw his clipboard across the table and yelled, "What the f— were you thinking?"

Marc was particularly perturbed because Anna had been making great strides, and doing this had set her almost back to square one. This may not have been what Jung and Freud had in mind when it came to therapy, but it worked. Many times Anna has commented on the now-famous speech, saying, "I'm not doing anything to get the 'What the f— were you thinking' speech." I have to admit, there have been times when I have had second thoughts about what I was going to say or the way I was about to approach Marc. I, too, feared the speech.

He didn't just give Anna all the attention, either. He gave me recognition and respect. He never ignored me, and always listened to what I had to say. He once told me that I was Anna's greatest therapist because I saw her at home and out in the real world. Once I told him that all the E.C.T. did was irritate and complicate her condition, he stopped the E.C.T. treatment. If I told him that I thought a certain medication was causing problems, he would make an effort to change something. Most importantly, he was the only doctor in eight years that gave me hope. I asked him one day over the phone, "Will Anna ever get well enough to function again? Do I have any hope at all?"

Without a second thought, he said, "Well, yes… this is not permanent. There is always hope. I have seen a lot of it over the past twenty years. Women especially just seem to snap out of it as they mature. I don't know why, and it does not happen that way in every case, but most do. Don't give up. We still have a lot of miles left before we consider quitting."

Hope… there it was… like an old friend I had not seen in years. For the first time, hope presented itself, and Marc had given it to me. I am almost sure that if you were to ask Marc about his role in Anna's life, he'd just tell you that he was doing his job. If doing his job means going above and beyond the call of duty, then yes, he was doing his job. I think he was much more than a psychiatrist earning a paycheck and a living for his next tee-time.

He took the time to get Anna's medication correct. There is no exact science in prescribing medication, but he was determined to get the right mix. He took time to take Anna on as a patient, and she was no peach. He was personable with Anna and talked about the Jewish faith – not because he was looking to convert her – but because Anna's father was Jewish and she wanted to know more about the Jewish people and their customs. As a direct result, our family celebrates Hanukah as well as Christmas. But more than anything, he gave Anna hope too. When she was at one of her darkest places, she told Marc that she wouldn't blame him if he didn't want her as a patient anymore.

"I am here for the long haul and I am not going anywhere," he said, looking her square in the eye. "I think you are worth it, and as soon as I can get you to believe that you are worth it, you won't need me. I intend to see this through."

This conversation was the turning point for Anna. The words he spoke were words of life, hope and validation. From that point forward, her steps toward recovery began. Yes, he is a cantankerous little Jewish banty-rooster, but his heart is made of pure gold. He is far from perfect, but he is a good, decent member of the human race that could see beyond himself to meet the needs of fellow humans.

I don't really believe in luck, but I do feel lucky for the relationship Anna has with these two. I see now that it was a matter of grace and faithfulness of God that we were so fortunate to have Marc and Judy in our lives. I don't have words to describe my feeling of gratitude for their unwavering commitment to the crazy lady I was married to.

Without them, the following chapters of our lives would not have existed. In the end, it was not the prescribed medications or the therapy sessions, hospital visits or day groups that made the difference in Anna. Ultimately, it was the prescription of the best medicine ever – hope. Marc and Judy administered hope, and that is what carried Anna to wholeness.

CHAPTER 28

Sludge

I waited patiently for the Lord;
He turned to me and heard my cry.
He lifted me out of the slimy pit, out of the mud and mire;
He set my feet on a rock.

--Psalm 40:1-2

Psalm 40 describes a "slimy pit," a pit of "mud and mire." I always thought that it was a description of sludge. The sludge I imagine is mud and icy snow mixed together. I found some sludge once in the Pacific Northwest. I drove my Jeep Cherokee right into it. Actually, I slid off the icy road into the sludge because of my superior southern California driving skills.

I had never driven in ice and snow, so when I set out for the evening, I did not bother with snow chains or anything useful like that, I just drove. Ten minutes into the journey, I made a left turn. Well, the wheels turned left, but my Jeep continued moving straight forward. I slid sideways into about two feet of a wonderful concoction of murky hell – sludge. I sat there revving my engine, trying to build up the power to get out of my dilemma.

The first and only rule of sludge: Sludge makes things stuck.

I sat there just revving and revving, hoping to get out, but to no avail. I had to get out because I didn't want anyone to know that I had gotten stuck. My pride didn't want people to know that I was just a silly California kid with absolutely no winter driving skills. So I pressed the accelerator and I sunk deeper into the sludge.

Oh, it gets better. I decided that I could make use of my new Maglite and I went to survey the situation. Let's review. The first rule of sludge is, "Sludge makes things stuck." Okay, remember that.

I stepped out into the night, into the cold, wet muddy ground. Once one foot was in, I thought that it would be okay to stick the other foot in, too, since I was now committed. Muck was halfway up to my calves. I took a step, and of course, remembering the first rule… I was stuck, and moving my feet only caused me to lose my balance and – *splat!* I fell face-first into the mucky goop and my new Maglite torpedoed into the mud. I let out a few colorful words. Now everything was stuck. Only after rolling around in the mud and mire for a full five minutes did I manage to get to one knee and eventually stand up. I looked like I had been wrestling an invisible greased pig.

"At least no one saw this comical display," I thought. I was dead wrong. As I stood to my muddy feet, I saw two of my neighbors staring at me. After they finished laughing, we managed to pull my Jeep out of the mud and onto the icy road. I drove home in my bare feet and underwear, making sure that I did not go faster than five miles per hour. It was only a four-minute drive, thankfully. I never did find my brand-new Maglite.

Sludge makes things stuck. We were stuck there in a pit, the place of hopelessness, the place of despair. "The Pit" was the address Anna and I lived at for years. It was fitting to refer to the 975 square-foot apartment we lived in as The Pit. The Pit was best fit for two people, three at best. We crammed all five of us in that pit, and somehow made it a home. We used to joke that you had to be careful not to trip in the bathroom or you'd fall out the front door.

The Pit I am referring to was not our physical address. It was our emotional address. I am talking about the pit of despair, depression and hopelessness; the sludge of suicide, self-cutting, blood, death and mental torture; stuck in bitterness, anger, betrayal and fear.

The description of Psalm 40 is not being "stuck in the mud." Psalm 40 is about being pulled out of the mud. If you haven't figured it out by now, I like Psalm 40. In fact, it has become our theme.

When Anna first realized that she was depressed, before her official diagnosis, she had a vision of herself being in a pit... a deep hole in the ground with no way out. A hand reached in and pulled her up to safety. Anna thinks this way. She is very artistic and she thinks in word pictures. She has been known to paint those pictures.

Anyway... the day she had that mental picture, she read Psalm 40. From 1996 to present day, Anna has kept a tight grasp on this portion of scripture and that mental image. The day she read it, she came to me and read it aloud. I had heard it before, and at the time, it was pretty much just another verse from the Bible. I know, I know... I can be such a clueless wonder! It would be years before I would see the real value and meaning of this verse.

The sludge loosened. Anna was pulled from the pit. I am not sure what made the biggest difference. It could have been the years of therapy or Marc's "What the f— were you thinking" speeches, or maybe it was the medication, but one day, she changed. Someone or something pulled her from the pit. Or maybe she climbed out – maybe both. But something shifted. It was a random, out-of-the-blue moment.

I was peeling potatoes in the kitchen that afternoon when Anna came to me and said, "I want to take a class." I was surprised.

"What kind of a class?" I asked, looking over the top of my glasses, still peeling potatoes.

"It's an EMT class. It costs $100."

I remember this very clearly. I sliced right through a potato once the words hit me.

"Uh… EMT. Did all those rides in the back of an ambulance get to you?"

We looked at each other and laughed. Maybe you don't see the significance of this, but it was *huge*! Anna had been stuck for so long that the only thing that mattered was winning the fight and getting over depression. She did not have a purpose other than seeking wellness. Now she was looking for a purpose outside of the illness. In the dimension of the unseen, I could hear a distinct sound of someone's foot popping out of the mud. The sludge had lost.

Anna progressed to a place where overnight stays at the hospital were no longer needed, and Marc placed her in the day program. A van would pick Anna up first thing in the morning and take her to the hospital. The day program was group therapy and other sessions from 9 a.m. to 2 p.m., and then the van brought her home. The evening of her last session in the day program, Anna began EMT school.

I want to make sure that I give credit to whom credit is due. Truth be told, it was a combination of Marc, Judy, the medication, the endless therapy sessions, and the hospitalizations. Hundreds of people who did countless random acts that contributed to Anna's newfound purpose and wellness. These unsung heroes helped Anna find hope and belief that one day she very well could be free from the sludge of the pit.

With hope confirmed, Anna and I hung onto the possibility of wholeness. My faith was wrung out, and I was filled with doubt and fury. Anna, however, knew and believed that if she was ever going to overcome this illness, it had to be with the help of God Almighty. I can't recall one instance when Anna asked why God was letting this terrible illness happen to her. Not one time did she ever utter a negative word about her faith. The worst I heard was, "I wish God would make this all go away."

What happened was nothing short of a miracle. The theme of Psalm 40: 1-3 is not about being in the pit. It is about someone getting us out of a pit. "He heard me… He lifted me… He set my feet on solid ground." Verse one says, "I waited patiently on the LORD." He is the "He." The Lord pulled Anna out of the pit. The mental picture Anna had years before of a hand reaching in and pulling her out of the mud and mire looks to have been a glimpse of the future.

The race that began in 1996 was in its final turn. The journey that started in 1970 was coming to its destination of purpose and hope in 2004. Anna was out of the pit and on her way to becoming an EMT, and it was all God.

When Anna saw Marc for one last official visit, she asked to be removed from the day program altogether. Marc granted the request with great joy. As he signed the paper, he said, "I was wondering when you were going to ask."

On Anna's last day in the program, they held a little graduation ceremony where therapists, nurses and Marc presented Anna with a diploma. It was October 2004 – eight years since her first admission to the funny farm. For eight years, Anna had been a fixture in this hospital, and now it was over. She had won; we had won. Anna drove herself home that evening and fixed dinner for her family. However, that evening, Anna would not be at home. She would not be available to tuck her children into bed. No bedtime stories, no bedtime small talk with me. She would once again make a choice that would take her away from her family. That night, Anna attended her first class in EMT school.

CHAPTER 29

Hero

It was quite a spectacle for my family to see the woman we knew as "the crazy lady" become an EMT. We all called her crazy, and that was our family's way of adding a little levity to a serious situation. Remember, our family is sarcastic and dark, and so making fun of Anna's illness was just our way.

Now the "crazy lady" was on her way to becoming an EMT, but it didn't come without some tribulation. Anna had a lot of self-doubt, and I think she tried to quit the class a few times. This was largely due to feeling inferior to the rest of the people in her class who were mostly half her age.

The E.C.T. treatment had done a bit of cognitive damage. Anna's ability to comprehend what she read, and even just simple memorization was quite a challenge. She was an honor student in high school and never had to put any effort at all into remembering facts, but now that she'd had her brain zapped a few times, things were different. Every single day, I listened to the self-doubt and her worries of cognitive damage. Every day, I encouraged her to press on.

Anna made three attempts to quit the classes. Our youngest daughter's school project curbed the third attempt. Rebekah was given an assignment to write a paper and paint a picture of a person she considered to be her hero. Most kids in the class picked Spiderman or historical figures, but Rebekah picked Anna as her hero. Just about the time Anna thought it was time to hang up the idea of becoming a paramedic, Bekah brought home the report and painting. I am staring at the painting at this very moment. Blue background with red crosses, an ambulance, hospital gurney, syringes and casts with the words painted in big, black letters:

"MY MOM IS MY HERO."

Yeah, how could she quit after that? It was the boost Anna needed, and she graduated a full-fledged EMT after passing not only the class, but the National Emergency Medical Technician board exams. It was amazing to watch my once-wounded wife become the healer. I was so very proud and excited.

What do you say to a person who was once ready to quit life, but overcame every obstacle and turned it around to embrace life? She battled many villains and won. She battled the sludge and won. She battled abuse and won. She even battled mental illness and managed to remain a wife and mother and become an EMT. Real heroes don't wear tights and capes, they wear the scars and bruises of survival. Real heroes have bled, and know first-hand what life's villains can do. They have stared them in the face and beaten them. That is why my best friend, my partner, my wife is my hero!

The naysayers have called me stupid, weak, unrealistic, and have accused me of being addicted to tragedy. I have been called co-dependent, self-hating and even self-abusive. People tried to label me a bad parent for allowing my children to be around their mentally ill mother. I have been gossiped about, and brutally convicted in the minds of those who don't know anything about me or my family, accused of lacking the ability to make sound judgment because I stuck by my bride.

They couldn't see the end and I could.

I saw that one day this would be a story of victory and not defeat. I saw, Anna saw, and our kids saw that there would be an end to this story and it would make us people of strength, hope and love. In the end, it didn't matter what the negative people thought and said. We would rise above the pain and emerge heroes.

Anna is the hero of this story, and today, as I put these words down, she is out in the streets rescuing the wounded. Her best calls are the ones who have swallowed a bottle of pills or have attempted some horrible action to end their own suffering. She knows what to do and say. Her co-workers shy away from the psych patients, but Anna takes them with great humility. The wounded became the healer; the downtrodden is now a facilitator of hope. It's a bit remarkable if you think about it.

Anna went to work as an EMT in the summer of 2004, and we became a normal, two-income family. We had survived the worst of the worst and all should have been well, except that there was a lot of damage that had been done. The aftermath was like being a shell-shocked vet after serving consecutive tours of duty. I was suffering from a sort of unofficial post-traumatic stress disorder.

I just kept waiting for the next bad thing to happen. I just knew that at any given moment, Anna was going to relapse and return to the hospital. I waited for the next step in psychosis to deliver its earth-shattering blow, and it did. Anna was not the psycho this time. I was. I was the one experiencing the flood of an emotional downpour.

First, it was just a quiet episode of self-doubt and feelings of hope-lessness and fear. Then, it was endless sadness and shame. I would burst into tears nearly every morning at the slightest hint of stress. Life had me by the short hairs, and I was sinking into the sludge that Anna had so victoriously escaped. I could curb my sadness at work by substituting my emotional struggle with anger. I could scream, yell and be angry. It was the acceptable and manly thing to do, I guess. Soon, the sadness was no more and it was just plain anger. I was angry at everything and everyone.

In the summer of 2005, the winds of change blew in my direction again, and everything that I thought was my future vanished in the single stroke of a pen.

CHAPTER 30

Winds of Change

Sometimes, just when you think you have it all figured out and you are sure things are going to be a certain way forever, the winds of change blow in your direction and nothing is the same. Nothing is the same and everything is different.

"I'm not supposed to tell you this, but there are going to be huge cutbacks, starting with a layoff this Friday, and you are on the list," my immediate supervisor informed me. The corporate office was making cuts and I was in the first wave of people to lose their jobs. There was nothing anyone could do about it. "Well, isn't that just the pickle on the crap sandwich that is my life!" I said to my boss, trying to bring a little levity to the conversation.

I had worked in ship repair for a long time and I sat there staring at my boss, realizing that all my security, dreams and future were going right out the window. I was supposed to be on the fast track to becoming a future project manager. I was a rising star within the company… so I was told… so I believed. As it turns out, I was just a number on a page, and when push came to shove, no one went to bat for me. No one had the power to stop the inevitable. I was unemployed on a warm Friday afternoon in September, 2005.

Funny thing was, Anna didn't flip out and go back in the hospital.

I was losing my mind with all the fear and doubt, and that, mixed with a little resentment, made for a nice concoction of, "Oh my freaking God, what now?!" But Anna (the psych patient, remember?) remained calm, and she just reminded me that we had made it through worse and we would make it through this.

We did. I received a sweet little severance package. I found another job in a small shipyard in town, but I didn't stay there. I thought that I would stay in San Diego, continue my career there, work in a small shipyard and that would be that. It was nothing like that. Everything went into hyper-crazy mode and things began to get out of hand.

I thought that I'd work in the shipyard, become a project manager, retire at sixty-five and live happily ever after. I thought that I'd save money, buy a house in San Diego, and have a life of sunshine and seagulls. Nope… wrong again. Not one thing that I thought was going to happen happened. All my plans, ideas and thoughts dissolved right in front of me.

By November 2005, we left San Diego and moved to Las Vegas, of all places. Sin City!

CHAPTER 31

Living and Loathing Myself in Las Vegas

W
e moved to Vegas in November of 2005 where I went to work building high-rises and Anna continued her career as an EMT. It was a fresh new start in a new city. It was exciting – the lights, the glamour and the buffets.

Las Vegas, billed as the entertainment capital of the world, is famous for the number of large casino resorts, their associated entertainment, and of course, gambling. The city's burlesque shows, strip clubs and all sorts of adult entertainment have earned Las Vegas the title of Sin City. So obviously, this is the place where people go to find God, right? You bet it is!

I wasn't really looking for God. In fact, if anything, I was trying to lose God and get Him off my trail. No such luck. When I got to Las Vegas, all the debris and fall-out of the previous years had settled in my heart and festered into a gangrenous infection that turned me into a heartless, bitter, mean-spirited man. I did not walk around yelling and punching people, but I had a chip on my shoulder and I just dared people to cross me. I was not in a healthy place.

The last thing I wanted was church people or God anywhere near me. Oh, I still acknowledged God, but I didn't want to do what His so-called followers did anymore. My issue was not with God, but with His hypocritical, judgmental people.

I could not walk away from God. There were too many things in my life that I knew God had saved me from. I was on the rebound from seeing my wife healed from mental illness to wholeness. That was nothing short of a miracle, so I had to give God props for that. I was just tired of His jerk followers. I was determined not to be like them or be near them. Then a couple of things happened that changed my thinking.

November 17, 2005, Elaine died. Elaine had been diagnosed with stomach cancer nearly a year earlier, and after a battle, the cancer dealt its final blow and Elaine passed away. I am not sure exactly how to describe my feelings about one of my dearest friend's death, other than to say that a world without her was a sadder place to live. It also made me a sadder person because I lost more than I could possibly describe. If you recall, I went to Elaine's house when things went badly for me in the beginning of this story. We had a special friendship that seemed almost unnatural.

Our unlikely friendship developed because we served on the same church staff together back at First Church. Elaine was a church lady. She was raised in church, lived in church, and always served in the church. I was not a church person. I was from the outside and my rough edges seemed to offend Elaine at the beginning of our relationship. Even though I was a pastor, Elaine constantly corrected my somewhat rebellious and rowdy behavior. Because of this, Elaine was not my favorite person. She was too uptight and rigid for my liking, and soon my outrageous behavior became a game for me. I liked to say and do things just to get a rise out of her. She once accused me of swearing at a copy machine because I called it a "gosh-darn piece of crap." She ran – and I mean ran – over to me and told me that I was swearing and that this was not the type of language that a youth pastor should use. I laughed at her and told her that if she didn't leave me alone, I would show her what real swearing was. She stomped away with her nose in the air and I just laughed at her.

I am not quite sure when we settled our differences and became friends. It may have just slowly developed into a friendship, but we became very close. She was eighteen years my senior, so she was old enough to be my mother, but we acted more like siblings. I used to tell her she was just like the sister I never wanted. We were good for each other. She taught me the importance of godliness – how to be gracious, and how to maintain pride and still be humble. I taught her to be daring, a free spirit, and yes, I had her swearing when it was all said and done. Not really badly, but the fun words like "dang" and "heck." I could write a novel just on the adventures we had doing church musicals together. Friends like Elaine do not just happen. They are predestined and rare. I was so blessed and fortunate to have had a friend like her.

When I learned that her stomach cancer was terminal, I was afraid to call her. I picked up the phone a few times, but could not gain the courage to dial the numbers. I had separated myself from most of my Christian friends. My stupid bitterness had taken control of me, so while I was being angry at "church people," I disengaged from my real friends who were good people.

I finally did gather the courage to call her in October, 2005. We talked for about an hour. She was doing pretty well, and I told her that I would come and visit her in Arizona once we settled in Las Vegas. I looked forward to seeing her again. She was terminal, but she still had time, or so we thought.

Tuesday, November 22, my daughter Bree called me on my cell phone while I was at work.

"Dad, when was the last time you heard from Elaine or anyone in her family?"

"I talked to her last month. Why?"

"I got a message from Riana on Myspace, and…"

"Bree… don't tell me she is gone!"

"She died Thursday, Dad… the funeral was today."

We hung up and I stood there in shock and full of regret. My friend was gone. My friend that meant so much to me was gone. My friend that never once heard from my lips what she meant to me was gone. Possibly one of the loveliest people that ever walked the planet, who had shown me so much friendship and loyalty was dead. I was in a solid state of mourning in a single second. Tears fell from my eyes in a downpour of pain. My spiritual temper-tantrum had cost me more than I could afford. I was not there for Elaine and her family in the last moments of her life. I was brooding and pouting, and I let my friendship with Elaine and with most of my other Christian friends slip away. Now I stood crying, regretting and hating myself for what I had done. I did it to myself. I had done it this time. I blew it.

She always helped me realize the right thing to do. It would seem that even in her death she would guide me back to the right thing. For with her passing, I began to realize my crucial errors in judgment about church, church people and spiritual wholeness. That afternoon, through the pain and regret, I felt a need for God again and prayed a heartfelt prayer for forgiveness and help.

CHAPTER 32

The Ultimatum

In the spring of 2006, I received a life-changing ultimatum. "Rudy, my emotional and mental stability is directly connected to my spiritual stability, and we need to go to church," Anna informed me with great resolve. I decided that I was not going.

"So go to church. I don't care," I said with my own resolve.

She looked at me with her eyes fixed on mine like a sharpshooter taking aim.

"I am going to church and you are going to take me," she fired at me. "In fact, we are all going."

"No, I am not, and that is final."

So there I was the next Sunday, sitting in church, thinking to myself, "I am the head of the household, but let's face it. At times, she is the neck that turns the head." I am good with that because she is right most of the time.

We visited a church close to our house, and I made it my job to criticize everything – the sermon, the music, the singer, the décor and the clothes the people on the platform wore. I made the experience as difficult as possible. Okay, the truth be told, the music was not very good and the message was generic at best, but I did not need to be the one who pointed out every fray in the carpet. I made the experience as miserable as I could. I was a real jerk.

It didn't take long at all, like two or three visits, before we were sleeping in on Sunday mornings and going to church was just a fleeting thought. Anna didn't really like that particular church either, but my constant criticism made it worse.

Still, Anna was very serious, and she meant every word she said about her stability being interwoven with her spiritual well-being. I knew that it would just be a matter of time before we would be back in church, and I'd have no choice but to go. Again, I remind you that I do wear the pants in this relationship, but I am in a twenty-year relationship with a stubborn person who embodies the very essence of being, in biblical terms, a stiff-necked Jew. No… I am not slinging racial terms here. If Jesus used the term, then I can use it too. I know when to just give in and do what she wants. It is, of course, the natural order of a thing… isn't it?

February 1, 2006, Officer Henry Prendes died. He was a decorated officer with the Las Vegas Metro Police. I never met him, but his passing would be a monumental event in my life. His death was nothing short of disturbing. A police officer in Las Vegas was killed in the line of duty, and it rocked the city. It was not just that a peace officer had died, it was the circumstances of his death. He had been shot and was already down. A few minutes later, he sat up and the assailant walked over and put one more fatal slug into him. It was a senseless death. The story hit a little too close to home with me because my sister is married to a highway patrolman.

The funeral was televised, and Anna happened to catch it by accident. Just to make this story hit even closer to home, Officer Henry Prendes was a Christian and was a member of Central Christian Church. Something about that funeral sparked Anna's interest in

Central Christian Church.

After Elaine's passing, I was shaken to the core. I was full of regret and sadness, and I knew, I just knew, that I needed to reconnect with God and His people. I needed to know the truth about the truth. I knew that there was a God. I knew that He loved me, and I knew He had saved me from myself for the past several years. Everything that I had seen in church and church people was false, judgmental and hateful. All the church, its leaders and its followers had shown me was contempt and mean-spirited words and actions. I figured, "Screw them! I don't need them, but what I do need is the truth." Where was the church that was more concerned with people and less concerned with their rules and ceremonies? Where was the church that was like Jesus Christ? Jesus said He was "the way, the truth and the life."

I began to pray again, but this time I just talked to Him. There were no special times where I got down on my knees and no limits set on how long I had to pray. I just talked. I asked questions and I listened. I usually heard nothing. However, I felt something. I felt Him there with me while I drove, while I worked, and especially when I was alone. There was no "parting of the red sea," no deep voices from heaven, just a presence.

No time before had I ever felt His presence. I figured that I was either going completely schizophrenic or something genuine was happening. At first, I went with schizo and just came to a sort of quiet resolve that I had finally flipped. I soon came to realize that there was something spiritual going on. It was quite possible that it was God, His spirit, with me.

I used to ask God to show me if a church actually existed that looked like Jesus; that actually cared about people. I wanted God to prove to me that there was a church that embraced their humanity, right where they were living, no matter how imperfect. I told God that if there was such a place that would be the church I would be a part of. I told God that His people had failed miserably and they were mean, judgmental, ugly, and that they completely misrepresented who Jesus was.

Maybe He agreed with me because He didn't zap me and kill me for saying that. In a way, I dared God to show me a church like that. I didn't believe that one existed and I doubted that I would find one in Sin City. I was wrong. I made a wager with God and dared Him to show me a place that was like Jesus. He took the bet, and I was getting hustled every step of the way. When God goes to Vegas, He goes there to meet people right where they are. He was about to win my bet, but I would get the payoff and hit the proverbial jackpot.

What I did not realize was that God goes to Sin City; in fact, He loves this place! He is everywhere you go. Peering over every bright light, every nudie billboard and strip club, there is God, looking, waiting and watching. He is in Las Vegas… *everywhere!*

When God comes to Vegas, He is up to something. He is up to His old tricks, seeking and saving the lost. When God goes to Vegas, the odds are all in His favor. The deck is stacked and He is the dealer, the house and the bank.

CHAPTER 33

Safe!

T he air was cool and crisp as I stood on my front porch, sucking on my third Camel cigarette. We were going to church this morning and that meant that I could not smoke for a few hours, so I made an attempt to overdose on nicotine before I left the house. Going to church made me a little nervous, but the idea of sitting there jones'n for a cigarette made it a horrifying idea.

Central Christian Church is a big brassy-looking building that could be a spaceship or a civic center. I sized up the building as we pulled into the colossal parking lot that came with a team of volunteers to direct traffic and park cars. One of these volunteers was jumping and spinning, doing flips as he waved his directional flags. He seemed to be enjoying his job a lot. Maybe too much. Our family drove past him and no one said a word, we just watched his parking lot acrobatics. My son looked at me through the rear-view mirror and said, "Okay, I've seen enough… Let's go home."

All of us burst into laughter and I replied, "As long as no one inside is doing acrobatics we should be alright, and if they are… I will race you all to the car!"

We made our way to the church. There were literally hundreds of people walking to and from the building. Most of these people looked normal, sporting jean shorts, t-shirts and flip-flops. The acrobatic parking attendant faded in our minds as we cleared the lot and hit the sidewalk. There was the smell of tobacco wafting in the air, and I looked around to see who was smoking at church. What I saw blew my mind. This was a church with a smoking section outside. I had been at churches that had people who complained that they found cigarette butts in the parking lot, and here were people outside smoking! At least I knew that if I had a nicotine emergency in the middle of service, I had a place to go.

As we walked by the "holy smokers," Anna looked at me and said, "Don't even think about it, pal."

"I wouldn't dream of it."

"You shouldn't lie at church." She knows me all too well.

As we entered Central, there was the smell of coffee lingering in the foyer. To the right was a bookstore and coffee shop that had a Starbucks quality in the décor. It also had a very Starbucks-like quality in the coffee, which we were allowed to take into the service with us! I am a coffee fiend, so this was like a little piece of heaven for me.

After being seated in the auditorium with our café lattes, I began to take in the room and all the people. Anna and the kids read the program. It was not like being in church. This was more like being at a convention or a rock concert – people milling about, talking and laughing, and music playing overhead.

"What have I gotten myself into?" I thought to myself. I was not uncomfortable, but I was wary of what might happen. I knew absolutely nothing about this church or their beliefs, so I was ready to grab my family and flee if this turned out to be some sort of cult or coven. After another survey of the people, I decided that so far, everything seemed normal and I could relax. I settled into my seat and read the program.

The program was just like any other church bulletin you might find in any church across America: youth meeting times and dates, upcoming mission trip info, blab, blab, more church stuff, blab, blab. I could hear Stevie Ray Vaughn's "Crossfire" playing, and I was very excited to hear a secular song in church, but this was the blues! When I looked up, the band was playing it live and it sounded incredible. I leaned over to Anna and said, "Well, the music is good." We had both thought it was a CD, but this wasn't Memorex, it was live!

The two-sided jumbo screens flashed advertisements for Starting Point, the membership class, next month's teaching series and witty little messages that reminded us of sales in the book store and not to speed in the parking lot. The next slide that popped up on those screens pierced my heart and soul. It was just a slogan:

Central Christian Church... Where it's okay not to be okay.

I was not okay. I was far, far from being okay. Not only were there the obvious problems with bitterness and anger, but I was guilty and ashamed. I was not passing through time oblivious to what I had transformed into. I knew exactly what I was. I was a former pastor who once had a deep passion for people and the Word of God. I used to believe that everyone deserved one good chance. I used to preach, teach and love the Bible. I knew the love, forgiveness and grace of Jesus Christ. Above all else, I was a compassionate man who loved people, and now I was the opposite of all that.

I was a former pastor who thought he had soured like milk sitting on the counter too long. I believed that there was no possible way that I was ever going to be able to go back to the way I was. I avoided all my old ministry relationships because I was ashamed of who I had become. My biggest fear was to be seen by a former member from one of the churches I had served. In short, I was scared of church people.

As I sat there in that auditorium, all I could think about was that if these people only knew that I was a former pastor, they would all think that I was a failure, a loser and a moral reject.

I was not okay, but according to their slogan, it was okay. God was there, too. It was as if God was kind of standing there with His arms crossed, looking at me, saying, "Well, what now, smart guy? Is this not the place that you told me did not exist? Are these people accepting enough for you? Are these people doing it like Jesus did? Well, c'mon, what do you have to say for yourself now?"

The pastor introduced the speaker that morning. I laughed in spite of myself as the message of grace and hope was delivered by Mr. T, of all people. God was probably laughing at me as one of my childhood heroes preached. The only way that morning could have been better would have been if Batman had been the special guest. I was blown away.

God won the bet. He showed me something I thought I'd never see, and there in Sin City, was a church doing business the way Jesus did. It was about saving lost and broken people with all their imperfections. No matter how sinful, degenerated, grotesque or damaged, people there were accepted and offered a place for healing and fresh starts.

Oh yeah, I was one of those lost, degenerated, grotesque and damaged people, and I found healing and a fresh start, which was the ultimate payoff. To keep in theme with Las Vegas and Sin City, I hit the jackpot. I was safe. I was home.

CHAPTER 34

Graffiti

Not too long after my first visit to Central, I saw the words that triggered this book. There I was, living in Las Vegas, a former pastor from California, working in construction, confused, angry, unsure, but willing to know the truth. Right in front of me was written in big fat letters with a Sharpie:

"Is this all just a joke, or is God doing this to us on purpose?"

I stood there staring at the question, repeating it over and over again. I thought to myself, "What did the author of this question mean? Was he serious?" I felt strange as I read the question again. Stupid graffiti written on an outhouse wall was having an effect on me that I could not control. I thought for a second that I might either cry or scream.

"I am on a construction site! I can't cry!" I thought as I looked around to see who might witness my apparent mental breakdown. "I can't really scream, either. What is going on? What is happening to me?"

I had an epiphany. The question written in Sharpie on the portable toilet was what I had been asking for over five years. The graffiti embodied my thoughts and feelings.

The question led to a quest, and I set out like Frodo going to Mordor. I threw off everything that I knew about God, the Bible and church and just scrapped it all. I started over. I started with, "Is there a God, and if so, does He really love me? Is His Bible really God's word, or is it just some ancient, irrelevant book like the atheists say it is?" Answers to these two questions came to me after a long, long thought process and study that took about, oh… six to seven minutes. I knew and believed that there was a God who loved me.

Still, I went to every atheist website imaginable, and I read it all. I read their ideas, philosophies and articles, just to see what other people were saying. I was looking for truth, and if the atheists did not believe that there was a God in heaven, I wanted to know why and see if I could put as much of my intellect into my beliefs as I could my heart and soul.

I do have the greatest respect for the entire atheist movement because they engage their whole intellect into their research. They are passionate about what they don't believe in. It shames the Christian community a little bit for our lack of passion. We do believe in a living God, and sadly, the Christian world is not as excited about this as we should be. I give big kudos to the atheists for their tireless work to prove God false. I just wish they were not so malicious toward people of faith. I certainly do not have ill will toward atheists and honestly, I don't believe God does.

After researching the atheists, I went to basic apologetics, and I read everything that I could get my eyes on about the subject. I discovered that I really didn't know crap about what I believed in, but between the atheists and the great Christian thinkers, from Francis Shaffer to Lee Strobel, I figured it out.

With a stronger foundation about who God is and what His word says, I attacked other questions like:

- Why is church important? The people there usually just piss me off anyway, so why go there?

- What is the truth about my political views? Can a person have liberal views and still be a Christian?

But the most important question I wanted an answer for was:

- What does Jesus really think is important?

I am not going to get into all the paths and roads I went down discovering the truth about the Truth, but I did find it. I knew that you couldn't find truth without doing what the Bible said; I made a commitment to myself that I would go to church every single weekend. The Bible says that it is important, so I went to church.

This was a good thing, since I found a church where I could hide. At this point, even though I was feeling a lot better about church, I did not want to go to a small group Bible study, teach a class, or even go to a class. I just wanted to sit and soak it all in like a sponge. I had no need to be noticed, no need to introduce myself. I just liked sitting in the back row in my shorts and flip-flops with a large coffee in hand.

I was still gun-shy, meaning that I didn't trust one person in that church. Not the freaky jumping traffic controller, the greeters, ushers or the pastors. I liked them; I just didn't trust them. I liked all the people in the past at church, and they were the ones who had done so much harm to my family and me. Why stick my head out there if I was only going to get hit in the face with a shovel? I kept my face safely tucked into my coffee in the back row, where no one really noticed or bothered me.

On the other hand, I did not notice what was happening to me. As I sat there every weekend, my faith in church and church people was being restored. This was because I saw, perhaps for the first time, people of faith who acted like Jesus. I saw people who claimed to be followers of Christ actually acting like him. It was a strange anomaly. I don't mean that they were walking on the water in their swimming pools or turning water into wine, but they were acting with the same compassion and love that Jesus Christ did in the pages of the New Testament. Love was everywhere and not the superficial sticky crap that makes me want to punch people in the face. It was genuine acceptance, and the people were normal. I don't mean just the pastors, either. I mean the people sitting next to me, in the coffee shop and outside smoking. It was very refreshing and downright cool.

It took about a year or so, but eventually I dropped my guard completely because there was nothing to guard myself from. The chip on my shoulder fell off and was never seen again.

I find it a bit ironic that I used to walk around stating that my life was crap, and graffiti on a crapper wall was what grabbed me by the soul to send me back to a right standing with myself, my family and the world around me. A very gracious and forgiving God took the time to whisper in my ear, "Look over there," so I could see His graffiti. I guess you could say I "saw the writing on the wall," and now… I just look for opportunities to sort of whisper in the ears of my fellow man the same thing: "Look over there…" Hopefully, I can be the graffiti in their lives.

CHAPTER 35

The Truth is Out

It was a hot Las Vegas afternoon on the fifteenth floor of a half-built high-rise. The crew was discussing the past – you know, the "good-ol'-days-gone-by" stories. They were stories of their involvement in gangs in Los Angeles, shoot-outs on the north side of Vegas, narcotic selling, robbery, felony after felony. Everyone laughed at the stupid things they had done, but I was quiet. I listened, laughed and told the guys how stupid they were, but I did not share my story. Then, one of the guys asked me, "What about you, Rudy? Do you have a story?"

"Not much to tell," I responded.

"We all told our dirt! It's your turn."

I looked at the guys and they were all looking back at me, and I realized that these guys would not give up.

"You really want to know?"

"Yeah, we want to know," the crew responded, almost in unison.

"My story is a little different than yours," I said, as I sat on an old paint can, lighting a cigarette.

"What is so different about it, dude?" one of the guys asked.

"Well, it is the polar opposite of you all. You were all gang-bangers and went to prison, sold drugs and dated strippers and bought whores. I didn't do any of that."

Frustrated, the crew began rolling their eyes and throwing up their hands. One of the guys said, "Yeah, we know you are a family man. You got a house and pets and a little wife that you come home to every night. You are a regular frigging Ward Cleaver."

I laughed out loud. "Yeah, sort of," I said, grinning at the guys and feeling somewhat embarrassed. I said something that no one on this crew that had worked with me every day for almost two years expected to hear.

"Well, I used to be a minister. I am a former pastor, formerly the Reverend Rudy."

There was an uncomfortable silence. No one spoke. No one breathed. They just stared at me to see if I was kidding or not. But I didn't laugh. After about half an eternity, I said, "It's true." The guys began to chime in with various comments.

"You have got to be kidding!"

"I can't freaking believe it!"

"Well, I'll be a...."

"You are one of the meanest foul mouthed bosses I ever had… wow!"

I took a final drag of my cigarette and threw it to the floor, looking a little annoyed by the statement.

"Yeah, well, I didn't say I was nice, now did I? Look guys, that was a long time ago and it doesn't change anything. It is a part of my life that is over."

"Jeeeeeeeesus, Rudy… you didn't molest a kid or something and get kicked out, did ya?"

My face turned red and my lips tightened as I stared down the first-year apprentice.

"Oh my God!" I barked. "Are you friggin' brain dead?! *No*! I didn't molest anyone! Things happened and I quit, okay?!"

My narrowed eyes gave the cue for the guys to go back to work. They all hurried to their areas of the building to work, and I was left alone.

Did I blow their minds? Oh yeah I did. These guys were very respectful, and I didn't hear about it again. I got comments over the next couple of days like, "I think it's pretty cool you had the courage to tell us."

It was not courage. There was nothing heroic about it. I just got tired of hiding it. I had gone back to church and was getting back into the groove, but I was hiding my faith. It was time to just come out with it and be done. It felt great. By the way, I did apologize to the first-year apprentice for calling him the bouquet of names I spewed at him, and all was well.

This is where it started. Every day I was able to tell a little bit of my story and about the goodness of God. Some listened, some didn't, but I wasn't on a mission to make anyone listen. I was simply letting my story reveal itself. The funny thing was, I didn't even realize that I was doing it. I was telling people about God, His grace and His power, not because I had to. It was not even because it was the right thing to do. There was no spiritual window that opened, it just happened.

I did have a renewed faith, but I did not exactly have a renewed lifestyle. I still smoked, cussed, told dirty jokes and got angry. I didn't run out and get all cleaned up and quit smoking, stop swearing and speak to people in soft-spoken tones. I was still the same guy, and I was not about to be fake.

This proved to be surprisingly effective. These so-called hardened criminal co-workers of mine responded to my story with acceptance and genuine interest. I had my fair share of things to work through spiritually, but while I worked through them, I had a crew of guys watching. It was more effective than opening my Bible and reading all the salvation scriptures in the "scarlet thread of redemption." It was them reading God's graffiti, His message, that was written on my life.

I don't see too many of these guys anymore. We have all moved on. To set the record straight, not one of these guys came to church with me and gave their lives to Christ.

I wish I could have written an incredible story of a guy working in construction that reached out and won thousands of souls for Jesus. I just have a credible story of a guy that shared his faith; some of the guys listened and some were touched. That is it. It is not always up to the messenger. It was up to the author of the graffiti written on me, if you will, to transform lives. That is solely the occupation of God Almighty. I'm good with that.

CHAPTER 36

Out of the Ash

Getting my feet planted on solid ground was what I'd call the natural next step. I was not quite there yet. I was a lot better than I had been a year prior, but I still had a couple of issues to work through. The biggest and most difficult obstacle for me was unforgiveness. This was primarily because of the bitterness that was running through me like a virus. I hate talking about this issue because it makes me look like sniveling little whiner, which I am not. But I was dealing with unresolved anger, hate and ultimately, unforgiveness.

It was not until February 2008 that I honestly forgave Pastor Rich and the rest of the cast of offenders and was over it. In January, I sent our pastor, Jud Wilhite, an email just to tell him how much Central Christian Church meant to our family. It was just a note to encourage him, and I didn't expect much more than a "thank you." This started a chain reaction of events that catapulted Anna and me into a healthy relationship with church and church people.

I sent the email because Jud had shared that he just felt that we as a church could be doing so much for the city of Las Vegas. I sensed his heart for this city and the church. He had just made the difficult decision to lay off a majority of support staff, and his heart was very heavy. Anna had been bugging me to send him an email for a couple of months, and this was the perfect time to send an encouraging note.

I gave Jud an abbreviated version of everything that our family had been through, and I said that if it had not been for Central Christian, my family would be lost.

The next thing I knew, I was getting phone calls and emails asking me for permission to share my email with the church during the weekend services. Apparently, I did my job, and my simple note encouraged Jud and the staff and now people who attended Central as well.

A few weeks after the infamous email, Anna and I were honored to meet with Jud. Over a couple of lattes, we shared our whole story in stereo. It was a monumental moment in our recovery because he said something I didn't expect; something that closed the deal, and I was officially over the betrayal and hurt. When we told Jud about what had happened at First Church and how the affair and our personal business had been made public to the entire congregation, he made one simple comment: "We would have protected that."

When he said those words to us, I was healed. I don't really have some profound words as to why. I just was. A pastor, my pastor, had somehow restored in me faith and hope in mankind, as well as in church leadership. I don't know what it was exactly, whether it was a psychological, emotional trigger, but "we would have protected that" was the final blow that put my monster to death. The horrible beast was left lying on the floor of the church café… dead.

As Anna and I left that meeting, she looked at me and said, "They would have protected that." I smiled back at her and said, "I know." For some reason, we had finally won the battle of what seemed to be a lifetime of hurt. The bitterness was gone. It was over.

Over the next few weeks, I was able to forgive the biggest offender, Pastor Rich. I arrived at the place where I no longer needed anything from him. I didn't need apologies or phone calls, and I didn't need to speak my piece. I just released the offense. I was able to do this once I looked at Rich as a fellow human with weaknesses, faults and imperfections. Maybe, just maybe, I held this man in higher esteem than any man should hold another. Believing that a mere man is incapable of error or sin is unhealthy and irrational.

This does not mean that I would ever call the man up or go to coffee with him. I believe that we can deduce the character of a person by his actions. We are what we do. For this reason, I can clearly understand a fellow man, a brother in the Lord, and not approve of his behavior. I also have the power to come to the clear, unbiased realization that he is not someone that I want to talk to or be around. Just because we forgive does not mean that we have to reenter an unhealthy relationship. "Never cast your pearls before swine." Enough said. The next thing I needed to do was face my own regret and forgive the person closest to me… that is, I needed to forgive myself.

"Guilt is regret for what we've done. Regret is guilt for what we didn't do." That is a great quote. I wish I knew who said it so I could pay proper homage to a brilliant statement. By the time my head cleared and my heart mended, I was full of regret that led to feelings of guilt. Guilt was present for what I had done: the hatefulness, smoking, excessive drinking and things that I had said that are impossible to count. I had regret for abandoning my faith, for all those years I didn't go to church, but mostly for leaving the ministry.

I wished I had just left well enough alone and continued doing what I loved. Now, I was eight years in the future, and I hated myself for making such a bad decision. I wished that someone had talked me out of it. I wished that I could go back and change it all. I had to own up to my actions and decisions, and it was almost more than I could bear. I carried that guilt and regret for a long time.

I called Barry the day I realized I had so many regrets. I opened the conversation with, "Tell me something… what was I thinking and why did you let me do this?"

After a slight pause, he replied, "Was there really anything that I could have said or done to make you change your mind?"

"Probably not, but a tragedy of this magnitude has to be some-one's fault!"

"Hello… it was yours! Hello!" he sang at me.

"Yeah, yeah… I know. What do I do now?"

"Get over it and realize that you are still the same guy and you still have a purpose and that nothing has changed."

With that being said, I realized that I had to forgive myself. I forgave myself for being a human with emotion that sometimes betrays me. For the first time in my life, I gave myself permission to fail and just be me. I realized that yesterday's flames of bad choices, bitterness and regrets were nothing more than a pile of ashes today. I figured that I could live in the ashes or I could make a new fire. This time it would be a controlled burn that was healthy and encompassed the strengths and talents that God Himself placed within me.

The final revelation came as I drove my 16-year-old son, Aaron, to an orthodontist appointment. I was engaged in one of those father-son talks that had been prompted by a recent report from school. The report showed that he was failing a few insignificant courses like math, English and science. I took advantage of the opportunity of having a captive teen in my car, or what my kids call the "box of doom." This is a great place to force a conversation!

It was a conversation where I, the father, got to open with, "Son, I think you are screwing up." What concerned me about the talk was my son's gloomy outlook on life. He just didn't see why it mattered, since it was all going to burn anyway. Yeah, I know. A little harsh for a 16-year-old, but at the time, he had a very melancholy spirit. We had been talking to him about it for months. I decided it was time that I told him that God didn't make a mistake, and if he was here, there was a reason, and we can assume that it is all worth it. I shared Ephesians 2:10, which says that we have a purpose which was predestined long before we were born. His attitude began to change.

"I know that I have not been a good example of godliness over the last few years, but I am getting back to God," I said. "I hope that you don't think that I am a big hypocrite. I just don't want you to miss out, man."

Aaron sat there for a moment, contemplating what I had said, and then he spoke.

"No, I don't think that you are a hypocrite."

"Well, I appreciate that, dude," I said, feeling relieved.

"You see, I look at people and I compare them to animals," he said.

I listened, not knowing where he was going.

"You can learn a lot about a person once you see them for the animal they are."

He gave me a few examples, and I had to ask, "What kind of animal am I?" I was hoping to get a lion or bear or something. His answer was unlike anything I expected or could have made up.

"You are a little different because you are not a real animal."

I drove on, feeling a little disappointed. "So what am I?"

"You are a phoenix. You see, in mythology, a phoenix is a bird that at the end of its life, bursts into flames and dies."

"So, I am a flaming bird?" I was now more disappointed, and also confused.

Aaron continued, "That's not the important part. Out of the ashes, a new phoenix is reborn. That's you, Dad. You are a phoenix rising from the ashes."

Speechless, I parked the car; my eyes were filled with tears. I was trying to show him that it was all worth it, and he turned it all around on me and showed me that I was to rise out of the ashes. He had just directed me to my destiny. He proclaimed who I was.

In the loft above my desk hangs a picture of a phoenix rising from the flames. Every single time I see it, I hear my son's voice say, "That's you, Dad."

CHAPTER 37

Rudy 2.0

Stubborn, mean, outspoken, jerk, impatient, crass, caustic, rude, arrogant, sarcastic, a force to be reckoned with, bombastic and a real S.O.B. are just a few of the oh-so-wonderful adjectives that have been used to describe me over the years. I really am a nice guy… until provoked, and then it can be a little ugly – or as my wife calls it, "disturbing" and "unnecessary." I think I am a decent enough person who has good qualities, but I have had to come to know myself for who I am and what I am. I like me.

In the past, I tried too hard to be something that I was not. I was, of course, the Reverend D. Rudy Trussler, pastor and preacher. I wore a suit every Sunday morning and I played the part. I said the right things, acted the right way and taught what I was required to teach people in church. The problem with that suit-and-tie-wearing preacher was that that was not who I was, and I didn't believe half the crap I was teaching. I believed that the Bible was the infallible word of God. But I was teaching some things that were the fallible words of men.

I traveled through some dangerous and self-damaging territory, but the journey introduced me to that raw, untamed person who lived within my skin. I am not referring to things as simple as likes and dislikes, but the substance that made me who I am.

In the end, it was like going through a meat grinder, and after being squeezed and pulverized, ground and strained, a pile of humanity was lying there, raw and unseasoned. At this point, it was as if God announced in heaven, "There! Now I can work with this!" Then he began to put the finishing touches on this new and improved version of me. Rudy 2.0, if you will.

The best thing is that when it was all done, that pile of humanity was someone I liked. I like who I am with all the blemishes and imperfections. I like my dark sense of humor, my gift of sarcasm and my stinging tongue. I like that I swear when I am angry or mash my finger. I like that I am impatient, imperfect and a little irreverent. I like that I am fun, a good father and that I have been married for twenty-four years – to the same woman! I like my love for the human race as much as I like my absolute disgust in mankind's inability to be decent and humane. I like that I truly have a weakness for "chick flicks" as well as "action flicks," and that I am somewhat of a romantic. I like that I believe in a loving, forgiving God and that I have a genuine devotion to the Holy Scriptures.

I guess when it is all said and done, I like the new person I have become. I say this with the utmost humility. It was not I that brought me to the state of self-acquaintance and realization; it was Jesus Himself. He was the one who stuck by me and was faithful to me even when I was not faithful to Him. He protected me from myself and from the great harm I could have caused – not only to myself, but to my family. *He* forgave, *He* restored, *He* renewed. The phoenix arose from the ashes of pain and sorrow to become the new, whole person that I am today – not by my own strength, but by the power of God.

CHAPTER 38

Cardboard

Easter Sunday 2008, the band rocked a rendition of "Amazing Grace My Chains Are Gone." People began to file across the stage. Each person had a piece of cardboard in his or her hands. The cardboard resembled any piece of cardboard that could have been in the hands of a homeless person with the words of a message written on it. They were just simple pieces of cardboard with duct-taped edges.

The words written on the cardboard were just as simple as the cardboard itself – just simple words written in thick, black, bold letters. What made the cardboard and the words special were the stories that they so eloquently told.

One man walked on stage and held a sign that announced to the world:

- ADDICTED TO PORNOGRAPHY

He was not an actor; he was the real deal. He was an actual man who had struggled with pornography, and he had just shared his personal struggle with thousands of people.

An attractive woman walked boldly onto the stage and held a sign:

- RAPE VICTIM TURNED STRIPPER

One by one, people lined up across the stage, sharing their stories.

- ADULTERY SHATTERED US
- ADDICTED AT AGE 13
- ANOREXIC, BULIMIC

Sharing these personal stories and struggles was a selfless and phenomenal act, but what made the difference was what happened when the cardboard signs they all held were turned over to tell the rest of their stories.

The sign that said ADDICTED TO PORNOGRAPHY was turned over to reveal FREE AT LAST! Other signs said:

- RAPE VICTIM TURNED STRIPPER
    - HEALED, FORGIVEN AND A PASTOR
- ADULTERY SHATTERED US
    - GOD RESTORED US
- ADDICTED AT AGE 13
    - CENTRAL'S RECOVERY PASTOR
- ANOREXIC, BULIMIC
    - BEAUTIFUL BY GOD

You can probably imagine the tears and emotions that ran rampant throughout that Easter service. It was the testimony of testimonies. They were real people telling their stories of faith, hope, grace and the amazing power of God with graffiti.

There were two people with cardboard signs that stood out to me. The first was flanked by the Stripper-Turned-Pastor and the guy who was freed from porn. The man held his sign with a whimsical smile and looked like he might burst into laughter. His sign was not as exciting as his stage partners', but it was definitely near to my heart. The sign simply said:

BURNED BY CHURCH

He stood there and smiled and flipped his sign with great pride and revealed:

RENEWED IN CHRIST

For the average person sitting in that audience, this was probably the most unspectacular sign on stage, but it had everlasting value to me. There was no atrocity or addiction, no abuse, no moral failure, just a guy who was burned by the one institution that was supposed to be a place of hope, reclamation and above all else, restoration. The very idea of this guy being restored once again in Christ put a smile on my face. Hope was piercing the wounded souls of thousands.

The next person, a woman in her late thirties, held a cardboard sign which was possibly one of the most powerful signs on the stage. Her sign was also simple. It bluntly read:

ABUSED

ADULTERY

SUICIDE

Again, the words were read and in a single motion, she turned her sign to present the rest of the story with:

HEALED

FORGIVEN

ALIVE

The audience burst into applause as they did with every sign that was flipped, but hers was met with a thunderous applause of appreciation. I looked around and saw people with tears running down their cheeks and giving thumbs-ups.

If you think that these two people had distinct similarities to my story that is because the first person was me and the second person was Anna. We were asked to share a little piece of ourselves and our story and stand in front of a crowd of over 20,000 people that weekend with graffiti on our little cardboard signs. We don't know for sure if anyone saw us and felt hope, but maybe there was someone that struggled with the imperfections of church leadership and had been lied to and betrayed that read my sign and decided to give it another try. Perhaps a young woman was sitting in the crowd that had made several unsuccessful suicide attempts and didn't know if she would live to see the next weekend. There was Anna… healed, forgiven and alive. Maybe that was just the message she needed to cause her to call her therapist and live to see another Easter.

After all, that is all we could possibly hope for. Being a cardboard sign-holder that weekend was the final event in my life that set me straight. I preached my first sermon that day as the new and improved version of Rudy, and I never even opened my mouth. I shared a lifetime of hurt and healing with a cardboard sign and a little bit of graffiti.

Since that weekend, the entire world has changed for us. We got to sit and talk with other people who were holding signs and we were privileged to have an opportunity to hear them tell their stories. Every person was just as interested in our story as we were theirs. Each story was a testimony of God's grace and power. That weekend changed our lives forever.

Since then, we have just evolved into healthy, spiritual people who know who we are and what we believe and we know God in a very intimate and deep way. It's not spooky, superficial or dramatic. We have a very meaningful relationship with God and we yearn to know Him deeper every day.

In September of 2008, we became a part of the volunteer staff that opened a satellite campus in the southwest part of Las Vegas. Anna and I ran the prayer ministry there, and had the privilege of working with a team of believers that see people every Sunday that are beaten down and abused by the enemy of our souls. We prayed with them and sent them off a little better than they were when they walked in. It was an awesome and humbling feeling every time we met one of those people.

We had a weekly small group with a crew of people whom we love and appreciate very much. Our children are all involved in some facet of ministry at church, and each of them are hammering out their own relationship with themselves and God.

I have had the opportunity to share this story with a few different groups over the past few years. Every time I do, I am asked by at least one person "What happened? What really caused you to give up so quickly?" The questions used to paralyze me in fear because I felt judged. I soon realized that people asked because they needed to know. They were experiencing the same thing, felt trapped and needed a way out. I usually answer them with something like this. What happened to me can happen to anyone if you lose focus on what is true. I lost sight of the good things and focused on the bad. My perspective was clouded with fear. Fear gave way to negativity and that led me into insecurity and doubt. Once that took root, I was hopeless. Living with no hope opened me up to being deceived by my own thoughts. In short, I took my eyes off of God and became obsessed with all of my problems. The more I focused on Anna's illness, what everyone else said about me or did to me, the more I believed things about my life that simply were not true.

This brings me to the next problem. I pushed everyone away and chose to walk alone through the worst time of my life. I believed lies about myself and my situation. I didn't have anyone in my life that I trusted to tell me the truth. We have to have people in our lives that we trust more than we trust ourselves, that we know love us and have our best in mind. That way, when deception shows up, they can tell us, "Hey dude, you're not seeing this thing clearly." Life is too hard at times to try to navigate through solo. We have to have people around us to redirect us when we are about to go off a cliff.

The last thing I have to point out is His radical faithfulness. Even though I was not faithful to God, He stayed faithful to me. I didn't even think about God during that time but He was focused on me, protecting me. The father heart of God is awe-inspiringly good. It was hard to connect with the concept at first. I learned that I had so many misconceptions about God that I totally missed Him working in my life. The first thing was that I believed that God wanted me to do something, to perform or give Him something first. I believed that He needed something like a down-payment to bless me or love me. He does not require anything. He just loved me.

This is what blows me away. It keeps me up at night thinking about His great love for His children.

In that nearly eight-year time period, I was a mess. I didn't trust myself, much less anyone else. I was too broken, bruised and burned. He loved me, yes, but He also trusted me. He trusted me with my messed up life and all my anger and rebellion to do the right thing! He had faith in me! In the situation where I needed protection, He protected me. Most of the time, He protected me from myself. He protected my wife from becoming swallowed up in mental illness and He protected my kids from the devourer.

I was taught in my early Christian experience that when we came into God's kingdom, we were covered by God's umbrella of protection and blessing. He covered us until we did something wrong. Then the umbrella was removed and we were subject to illness, tragedy, hardship and ruin. Then we had to work ourselves back into God's grace.

But when I flipped out and walked away, He covered me! He protected me. He gifted me His blessing and protection and carried me until I was able to walk on my own. That is the goodness of God right there!

He carried us back after being strays for many years. He brought us home to His kingdom forever changed, renewed and whole. The fascinating part is that Jesus led us back.

"If a man has a hundred sheep and one of them gets lost, what will he do? Won't he leave the ninety-nine others in the wilderness and go search for the one that is lost until he finds it? And when he has found it, he will joyfully carry it home on his shoulders" (Luke 15:3-4).

No matter what your circumstances may be, God's business is reclamation. He is always looking for that one lost sheep, and if you let Him, He will pick you up and carry you home.

.

CHAPTER 39

Joke vs. Purpose

I t all started with graffiti and the story ends with graffiti. When I read the message on the port-a-potty wall, I had no way of knowing that my answer would come when I held a cardboard sign two years later. You remember the question that started all this:

"Is this all just a joke or is God doing this to us on purpose?"

To truly answer this question, we have to ask ourselves, "What do we really understand about God?" Does God laugh at our calamity? Is suicide, self-abuse, betrayal or addiction ever funny? Does God sit at some sort of cosmic control console, feverishly pushing buttons and throwing switches to make every single detail of life happen?

God does not make bad things happen, nor does He laugh at us. Life just happens. Disease, death, breakups, financial ruin, struggles and hardships are just a part of life, and to think that God has a hand in the bad things is just ludicrous. We forget that the real culprit is Satan. He is the thief who comes to kill, steal, destroy and torment us. Satan and he alone, is the bringer of the bad.

Here's what really happens. God uses the bad situation for His own good to bring you ultimate happiness and peace. Read John 10:10, the book of Job, the first chapter of James and the Psalms. Ultimately, God is on our side. He is our advocate and our deliverer.

Life just happens, and it is how we respond to it that makes the biggest difference. Sometimes there is a learning curve and sometimes there is not. In my case, there was. It was because of how I responded to my situation that my life took the path of bitterness and misery. I stopped trusting in what I knew was true and took matters into my own hands.

I deeply regret the time wasted. I spent years in anger, sorrow, loneliness and defeat that was not necessary. Looking back, it all could have been so much easier if I had only done things differently. For a short time as I wrote this, I was very depressed just at the thought of what I had done to myself. I realized that Pastor Rich and the entire cast of people that caused harm did not make me respond the way I did. I had to take responsibility for what I had done, and for the most part, it was no one's fault but my own.

I made a decision – a decision to never take my focus off God ever again, no matter how horrific the situation. I made a decision to forgive those who had wronged me and a decision to forgive myself. One morning, I read this in Isaiah 43: "Forget the former things; do not dwell on the past."

The final decision was to do exactly that. I let it all go and moved on. The end result was a stronger, more equipped person. I may have met God on the way up, but I really got to know Him on the way down.

This book is not about addressing why bad things happen to good people. It is to show you that God is there right now, whether you feel Him or not. He is real and is active in your life. An old Pentecostal preacher I used to listen to years ago always said, "What the devil meant for bad, God will use for good." You know, that ol' boy was right!

Don't focus on the bad; embrace the goodness of God Almighty. You might as well do it now, because waiting is just going to be a waste of time. Do you really have time to waste?

No, this is not a joke. God deeply cares for us and what happens to us. As for Him doing anything to us on purpose, well… yeah, He does do things to us on purpose. He blesses us, forgives us, rescues us, engages us and loves us enough to die in our place.

Life is going to happen, and it is going to happen hard. It will be mean, ruthless and devastating. Life will also be full of hope, love, happiness and good times. What we have to remember is that there is one that gives and there is another that steals. I love the New Living Bible translation of John 10:10: "The thief's purpose is to steal, kill and destroy. My purpose is to give them a rich and satisfying life."

"Is this all just a joke or is God doing this to us on purpose?"

Yep! You bet He is. His purpose is to give us a rich and satisfying life – a life of meaning, a life of hope and a life of purpose. And that, my friends, is no joke.

To wrap it up I will say this. The heart of the Father is Love. It is about relationship with him. It is not about compliance with rules, commandment or law. It's love. Yes, there are commandments but Jesus dying on that cross was an act of pure love to reconcile us to the Father. I am a father. It is my favorite title for me. I love my children. I never once just wanted my kids to merely comply with my rules and my ways. I want them to know me, to be like me and to love me. I want them to be influenced by me but I have never desired to control them. God the Father is the same. He wants us to love him and He wants us to come under his influence of love, because he is madly in love with you.

EPILOGUE

It has been nearly five years since Anna and I stood on stage with our signs. If memory serves me correctly, we shared the cardboard snapshots of our stories with close to twenty-thousand people on that Easter weekend. The significance of what really happened that day sent a shockwave through hell. We released the power of our testimony for the first time.

We are still telling our story to people everywhere. Every single time we share, the enemy loses his hold on people, his lies are dispelled and the power of God is released. Hope is restored. We have found that for the most part, everyone is looking for the same thing. It's hope. No matter how addicted, mentally ill or broken people are they just want hope. If our story can bring someone hope, we are committed to tell it all day, every day.

Today, Anna and I are back in full-time ministry. I once said I would never be in ministry again, but it would appear that God's amazing grace and plan for my life counteracted my empty threat. We are now the directors of a discipleship school in northern California. I have the privilege of teaching and counseling students from all over the world how to overcome lies and to walk in their destinies with freedom, power and authority. I wake up every day excited about what I do. I try my very best to model the Father's heart as I work with my students.

Anna heads up inner-healing, not just at the school, but also our church. She has an amazing gift of walking with people through the process of displacing lies in their lives with the truth of what God says they are. The wounded one has definitely become the healer.

Our kids are adults now and living their individual lives. My oldest daughter, Bree, and my son, Aaron, found their soul-mates and both got married this year. Bekah will be moving to Las Vegas to follow her dreams in the music industry. Bree is expecting her first child, which means adventures in grand-parenting will soon begin!

I don't really think about this story anymore. I don't think Anna or my kids do either. It doesn't make sense to look back at the mess when there is way better stuff up ahead.

We survived an elaborate assassination attempt orchestrated by the devil. But all of the mud he slung at us, all of the blood we waded through only made us stronger and wiser. Then one day, with cardboard signs, we carpet bombed hell with the testimony of what God's love and power can do. It was over. We emerged from the rubble, survivors — an unstoppable force to be reckoned with. I guess the joke is on the devil. We win!

3728968R00124

Made in the USA
San Bernardino, CA
17 August 2013